Dedication: ski the whole mountain

To all our clients who, over the years, have been our test subjects, sounding boards and friends.

THE GOODS

Acknowledgements   9

Introduction   12

Chapter 1: Essentials of All Mountain Technique   24

Chapter 2: Powder Snow   42

Chapter 3: Crud Snow   68

Chapter 4: Steeps   86

Chapter 5: Moguls and Trees   122

Chapter 6: Air and Other Secrets   136

Chapter 7: Backcountry Basics   158

Appendix: Drills for Skills   184

Information Page   191

SKI THE WHOLE MOUNTAIN

HOW TO SKI ANY CONDITION AT ANY TIME

by Eric and Rob DesLauriers

with photography by Hank deVre

MOUNTAIN SPORTS PRESS

Boulder, Colorado USA

Ski the Whole Mountain

Published by Mountain Sports Press

Distributed to the book trade by:
PUBLISHERS GROUP WEST

Bill Grout, *Editor-in-Chief*

Michelle Klammer Schrantz, *Art Director*

Alan Stark, *Associate Publisher*

Scott Kronberg, *Associate Art Director*

Chris Salt, *Production Manager*

Andy Hawk, *Sales Representative*

ISBN 0-9717748-3-8

Library of Congress Cataloging-in-Publication Data applied for.

Printed in Canada. By Friesens Corporation

A subsidiary of:

929 Pearl Street, Suite 200
Boulder, CO 80302
303-448-7617

ACKNOWLEDGEMENTS

Obviously, the most important acknowledgement goes to our parents, Ralph and Lynda DesLauriers. Thanks to our Dad for building and operating Bolton Valley Ski Area for so many great years. And thanks to our Mom for teaching us to ski and always focusing on having fun. At Bolton Valley we had the best childhood that either of us could ever have asked for. Thanks, Mom and Dad.

All of our lives we have had great skiers and coaches to learn from. Our first race coach, Craig Tighe, was one of the most natural skiers we can remember. Our uncle Chuck DesLauriers and his buddy Chris Lothrop were incredible skiers and the first guys to ever launch the big rock back home at Bolton Valley. Ian deGroot was another ski coach, friend and a key factor in shaping our skiing. (Good foosball player, too.)

Thanks to our ski brothers and sisters, the friends who have been there to push the limits and ride the lifts with us buzzer to buzzer on stormy powder days. To name a few: Tom Day, Kevin Andrews, Griff Davis, Allen Riley, Matty "Moo" Herriger, Kristen Ulmer and our brother Adam. Going back further: thanks to Erica deGroot-Lustgarten, Steph Riley-Sosnkowski, Garrett and Gabbie Valasquez, Robin and Grey Ricker and all the other "kids" we grew up skiing with.

Thanks to Tom Lane and Eric Perlman for getting us started in the film scene. And to our sponsors—Smith Sport Optics, Salomon, The North Face, Life-Link, Thule Car Racks and GU Energy Gel—for years of support.

A big acknowledgement and thanks to our X-Team Advanced Ski Clinic partners, John and Dan Egan and Dean Decas. The X-Team clinics are a ton of fun, and we see our clients getting better all the time. It has been in our X-Team clinics that we have developed our teaching methods and concepts.

Thanks to Harald Harb. Harald is a true maverick thinker and mover in a ski instruction industry that has been coasting along for many years. Harald helped us to focus on the movement of the inside foot. It was cool how everything we had been teaching for years in off-piste skiing just plain clicked with what Harald was doing.

And thanks to Rick Kahl, former editor in chief of *SKIING* Magazine from 1990 to 2001. Rick always gave us the literary leeway to write about instructional topics outside the mainstream.

Thanks also to Scott Kronberg at Mountain Sports Press, who did the design and layout of this book. Nice job, Scott. Thanks also to Seth Masia for his editing prowess, creating order from chaos.

A huge thanks to Bill Grout. Bill is largely responsible for the authoring side of our skiing careers. As executive editor of *SKIING* Magazine for many years, Bill got us started writing articles on advanced skiing topics back in 1994. We have been contributing editors ever since. Writing for *SKIING* Magazine was instrumental in the development of our teaching methods, because it made us structure our concepts. It's cool to look at the back issues of the magazine, because our articles basically chronicle the evolution of our teaching methods. Bill is also the editor and publisher of this book and a real motivating force behind it. Thank you, Bill.

Finally, we would like to give a very special thanks to our families for sharing our lives and making our time in the mountains more special. Thanks go to Eric's wife, Laura, son Wildon and daughter Emma. Thanks also go to Rob's wife Kit.

Soul time: Below the Couloir Rectiligne above Chamonix, France, Rob and Eric create plumes of powder in late-afternoon alpenglow. This view looks west from the Grande Montet toward the famous Aiguille du Midi cable car.

INTRODUCTION

The idea for this book started with a laugh. We were at Grand Targhee, Wyoming, in 1995, coaching one of our X-Team Advanced Ski Clinics. Our long-time client, psychiatrist Dr. Kurt, arrived in a flashy purple one-piece Bogner powder suit. But the loud suit wasn't what drew the heckles. It was his skis.

During a trip to Utah, Dr. Kurt had picked up a pair of chubby black skis. They spread out across the snow, wider than anything we'd seen before. Until then, we'd skied, raced, and taught on skis roughly 65mm wide at the waist. So had all our coaches, friends and students. Dr. Kurt's big fat lunch trays bulged 90mm wide at the waist. They looked like cartoon skis. No wonder we laughed.

But Dr. Kurt outskied himself that day. He ripped the pow. He was transformed from a normal, every-day psychiatrist into a superhuman mountain god (well...almost).

We had to try those skis.

And when we did, we stopped laughing. Over the next two years, we logged thousands of vertical feet exploring the limits of wide all-terrain skis.

Wide skis were a quantum jump. They made deep and steep skiing easier. Our turns became naturally rounder and longer. We skied faster, in all conditions. Our technique grew simpler—we needed fewer adaptive moves to deal with changing snow conditions. We skied more efficiently, with less effort.

Wide skis have changed the sport for everybody. Armed with wide all-terrain skis, ordinary skiers now routinely master snow and terrain that was accessible only to the best skiers in the world in 1995. Good skiers are now better than ever. Entire businesses have blossomed based on the wide ski. The helicopter ski operations in Alaska would never have gotten started without wide all-terrain skis. Heliski and snowcat companies in Canada, Utah and Colorado are fully booked, a year ahead of time, because wide skis rule on natural snow.

Doesn't it make sense that a wide, stable ski should work better in deep snow and crud? Back in the 1960s and 1970s, a few companies sold powder skis about 72mm wide. In Utah, for instance, the Miller Soft was popular among powderhounds, and the Rossignol Haute Route became a classic for off-piste skiing.

But mainstream ski designers had a really hard time moving away from the race ski as the primary design model. It wasn't until snowboarders began ripping up the powder bowls that ski engineers thought to go broader.

We had grown up on those narrow 65mm skis. Eric was born in 1963, Rob in 1965, both in Burlington, Vermont. In 1966, our father and grandfather, Ralph and Roland DesLauriers, opened Bolton Valley Ski Resort near Burlington. Our mother, Lynda, began teaching us to ski that year. The folks turned us loose to play in that huge, snowy back yard—5,200 acres of logged-out forest in Vermont's Green Mountains.

Eventually, we skied almost every day with a gang of about 20 kids. Half of them were locals (including our three younger siblings) and half were regular weekenders. By 1971 we were racing, coached by Craig Tighe, the son of Bolton's mountain manager. Craig had a strong, fluid style, which we emulated in gates and while freeskiing. Beginning around 1975, and right

WHAT IS A WIDE SKI?

Today's wide skis rip powder, steeps, and crud. They carve beautiful arcs on groomed snow, corn and windslab. They track through variable snow without porpoising. These skis reduce the balance variables required for sweet carves. This levels and opens the playing field for a ton of already good skiers to become a lot better. On wide skis, you can step it up and ski the whole mountain with poise and confidence.

We should define our terms. The typical wide all-terrain ski has a waist between 83 and 92mm wide, and a modest modern sidecut about 15mm deep. Since 1995, a number of skis have filled this niche, including the Atomic Heliguide, K2 Big Kahuna, Olin Outer Limits, RD Helidog, Salomon AK Rocket, and Völkl Explosiv.

As this is being written, in 2002, current examples include the Atomic R:ex (116mm at the tip, 84mm at the waist, 108mm at the tail), Blizzard Titan (120-82-103mm), Dynastar Inspired (117-89-110mm), Elan Mantis 777 (117-87-107mm), Fischer Big Stix 84 (116-84-103mm), Head Monster 85 (122-85-110mm), K2 AK Launcher (119-88-105mm), Kneissl Flexon Tanker (125-93-116mm), Nordica Beast 92 (124-92-116mm), Rossignol Bandit XXX (123-90-110mm), Salomon Pocket Rocket (122-90-115mm), Stöckli Stormrider DP (120-91-109mm), and Völkl Vertigo G4 (118-83-106mm).

The names and dimensions will change as ski design evolves, but the 85mm waist (give or take a few millimeters) will remain a common denominator.

Some lighter skiers won't be able to generate the G-load to hold the wide skis in an arc on groomed snow or solid crust. For these skiers, we recommend doing groomed snow drills with one of the 70-75mm all-terrain cruisers, then switching to wide skis for deep snow. Examples of this group include the Atomic R:10 and e:9, Blizzard Sigma K series, Dynastar Intuitiv 71 and Ski Cross 8, Elan Mantis M10 and Whisper 8, Fischer s200, Head Monster iM 70, K2 Axis X and T:9 Power, Kneissl Rail series, Nordica W71, Rossignol Bandit X, Salomon Scream 10 and Crossmax, Volant Gravity 71 and Vertex 71, and Völkl Vertigo G2.

---

through high school, we were coached by Ian DeGroot from the University of Vermont (UVM).

At age 13, Rob competed and the Eastern Junior Olympics and took home a gold in Giant Slalom, bronze in slalom and gold in the combined. Rob went to race NCAA Division 1 for Cornell where he graduated from the Hotel School. Eric attended the University of Vermont, graduated with a degree in Recreation Management, while coaching kids on the Bolton Valley Race Team. Eric coached his brother Adam who competed in the Junior Olympics during this time.

In 1986, our dad was planning to reno-vate the Bolton Valley base complex. He sent us on a tour of Western resorts. We were supposed to report on the village architecture. In Colorado, we hit Arapahoe Basin, Keystone, Copper Mountain and Vail. In Utah, we visited Deer Valley and Snowbird. Rob took his first real power pin-wheel tumble jumping a big cornice in A-basin.

Forget about architecture. The skiing opened our eyes. We abandoned all thought of spending our lives tucked away in New England.

We graduated from college in 1987— Rob from Cornell's School of Hotel Administration, Eric from UVM with a degree

When we were kids, we used to spend hours every summer pruning and thinning this area of Bolton Valley, Vermont (known as Devil's Playground), little knowing that our younger brother Adam and X-Team buddy Dean Decas would one day rip through there. Below: How do you say "yee-haw!" in French? Rob makes his first turn in the Couloir des Poubelles off the Grande Montet above Chamonix. Five thousand vertical feet below is the famed Vallée Blanche.

in ski resort management. Rob immediately took off on a trip around the world, making a stop at Squaw Valley en route. Eric hit Squaw in the spring of 1988. Down to his last nickel, he borrowed $50 to enter a pro mogul contest and won $500—enough to stay for another week. Then he went to Portillo, Chile, for the summer. Without a ski teaching certificate, he wasn't hired as an instructor. Instead, he talked his way into a job as the ski school video camera operator.

While circling the globe, Rob decided to spend a winter exploring the steep chutes of Squaw Valley. Eric arrived at the same decision. And we arrived at Squaw the day before Thanksgiving, 1988, in a huge blizzard. Pacific storms rolled ashore all through December, filling in the classic chutes of Squaw Peak's Palisades and Mainline Pocket.

We linked up with some of the local hardcore skiers, including Dan Egan, Giff Davis, Tom Day and Kevin Andrews. They showed us the great lines above Gold Coast and off Granite Chief Peak. By mid-December, Robbie Huntoon, recently former Squaw freestyle coach, got Eric signed up for the new Warren Miller film,

Extreme Winter. Truckee filmmaker Eric Perlman had just started his series of Skiing Extreme flicks for The North Face. Over the next 12 years, we averaged two films each winter.

We started coaching adult skiers in 1991, teaming up with John and Dan Egan and Dean Decas to form the X-Team Advanced Ski Clinics. Only six skiers signed up for the first clinic, but word spread fast. In the second clinic we had 60 clients.

In the early days, we based our clinics on our racing experience blended with our personal freeskiing styles. We knew what worked in race training, and we were open to trying anything that seemed to work in freeskiing development. Our clients were amazingly tolerant. We'd say: "You people are the guinea pigs for this new drill we're trying. Here's what it is supposed to help you do." And they'd try it!

Some things worked better than others, and by trial and error we evolved a set of teaching methods for a variety of situations. We still use this philosophy of openness and experimentation today, but our teaching methods are a lot more structured and simple now.

Skiing the whole mountain on straight, narrow skis required adaptation. We taught people to sit back a bit in powder, or to pressure the heel at the end of a short-radius crud turn. Lessons always focused on altering the pressure distribution to handle changing snow conditions.

Then in 1996—just as we were learning about wide skis—we got together with Harald Harb, then a member of the Professional Ski Instructors of America (PSIA) Demonstration Team. We found that everything we had been doing with advanced skiers, on difficult off-piste

BOLTON VALLEY ROCKS!

Bolton Valley is small, even by Vermont standards—it offers just 168 acres of lift-served ski trails. But it sits in the middle of 5,200 acres of logged-out forest, so as kids growing up there we found lots of backcountry skiing. And some of the race trails and mogul runs are surprisingly steep. We skied everything the mountain had to offer.

The key feature, for our gang of kids, was the Big Rock. It's a perfectly round 15-foot boulder right in middle of a run called Show Off. The rock sits right under the Summit lift, so when you make the jump, you always have a crowd. It was quite a show. All the best steeps can be found off this lift, along with all the best skiers.

The first guys to jump the Big Rock were our Uncle Chuck Deslauriers and his pal Chris Lothrope, in 1966, Bolton's opening season. The first time we did it, Eric was 11 and Rob 10. If it's a good snow year, you get about a 10-foot drop off the rock, but the first time we launched, it felt like a 1,000-foot free-fall.

This is Vermont, land of narrow, twisting ski trails. To survive a jump off the Big Rock, you had to land very precisely. Jump too far, and the landing flattened out. You'd absorb a hell of a compression, miss your turn and slam straight into the woods on the other side of the trail.

Our gang got very good at jumping the rock. We often launched in series, a dozen teenagers in a line, one right after another. You couldn't afford to splat the landing, because your brother was incoming half a second later. One way or another, we learned to stick our landings and ski away.

Off the cornice and onto the "Kitchen Wall" on the southeast side of the Palisades at Squaw Valley, California. Rob demonstrates a trademark of his skiing: A smooth, effortless style in the air.

Left: The mission of our X-Team Advanced Ski Clinics is pretty simple: Good times and good skiing. By the looks of this crew at Valle Nevado, Chile, we accomplished our mission. Blending in with the group are three X-Team coaches: Eric DesLauriers (left), John Egan (center between skis) and Dean Decas (second from right with shades on and goggles in stand-by mode). Right: Who said "Sierra cement"? And how often does cement float in the air like this rooster tail of deep fluff at Squaw Valley? Eric takes advantage of it.

X-TEAM ADVANCED SYNERGY

In 1992, with our partners John and Dan Egan and Dean Decas, we started the X-Team Advanced Ski Clinics. The "extreme" skiing scene was just getting going in those days, and the five of us were all starring in ski films like the annual Warren Miller film and the Skiing Extreme series produced by Eric Perlman. We decided to put together a series of ski clinics specializing in "extreme" skiing. It was, and still is, a unique breed of ski clinic. Who would have thought we'd still be cranking along 10 years later?

The synergy that occurs at our X-Team Clinics between the coaches and the clients, and among the clients themselves, creates an incredible learning environment. The combination of personalities and teaching styles seems to set people free to push their limits and become better skiers then they ever thought possible. As Dan Egan says, we help people to push through their "freakout" level.

We think the success has a lot to do with our love of the sport, our ability to share that love and our unique insights into the non-groomed skiing environment. We've taken clients to many great locations in the States, plus Alaska, France, Argentina, Chile and New Zealand. And we're not done yet. We still offer half-a-dozen locations per year. Come on out and join us.

Smooth moves. Notice how Rob's inside foot is light and how it controls the angle of the outside foot as well. He could be making this same move on a groomed run. In fact, the movement of the feet is exactly the same as it would be on a groomed slope.

terrain, corresponded with the movement patterns Harald was promoting as the Primary Movements Teaching System aimed at racing and freeskiing on groomed runs. The real magic—the common thread—lay in the smooth transition from one turn to the next. We had been encouraging students to lead this transition by relaxing pressure on the new inside foot. This was also Harald's main idea. We've adopted this as the key move for all-mountain skiing.

From that time on, two concepts flowed together: By using wide skis, and by leading the transition with a light inside foot, we could use the same technique on groomed snow and in deep, natural snow.

What this means is simple: Everyone can be a better skier. The movements and techniques we show in this book are easy to learn, largely because they feel good! When you get it right, you can feel the improvement instantly. You feel a smooth build-up of the G-force as your skis carve the snow. You can balance on one foot, or on two, as the pressure maxes out, or as terrain and snow density dictate. And you're balanced for an easy, flowing release into the next turn. Because the turn is clean, you exit in balance, so the transition into the next turn is effortless. The release of carving pressure has its own rhythm, and you arc back naturally into another smooth build-up of pressure.

The payoff comes with a seamless linking of one turn to the next (as opposed to the sensations of one good turn at a time). Both skis work together to form smooth round arcs.

Here's the real magic: A fundamentally sound groomed-snow technique will efficiently take you everywhere on the mountain. Groomers are a comfortable arena for practice and can give you something to focus on,

Eric arcs. Most of his weight is supported by his outside leg, but the inside is (riding in) parallel and poised for a smooth release into the next turn. Visualize a GS gate just out of the picture. See Eric atop the winner's podium.

especially early in the season when groomed snow is all you can find. Throughout the book we will look at most sequences from the fall-line of one turn to the fall-line of the next, or, to put it in another way, from the feel-good phase of one turn to the feel-good phase of the next.

Ours is not the only way to ski well. Frankly, there are an infinite number of movement patterns that can produce a good turn. Many really good skiers have styles radically different from the one we use and teach. We can often spot a ripping skier across the bowl and know who it is immediately by the unique style. Johnny and Dan Egan—total rippers—ski with a much different style than we do. They teach a different style, but still really help people to become better.

So, we are not saying this is the only way to ski or even that this is the best way. We do maintain that if you adopt our movement pattern as your base technique, you will ski consistently well and better, with less effort.

We call this a "clean" stance. Notice the snow coming off both skis, hands in front and eyes focused down the hill. Look at how the body position is so similar to the groomed-run picture on the facing page. Same basic stance, same basic technique, same basic Eric (in steep crud off a corner of the Palisades, Squaw Valley).

ALL MOUNTAIN SKI PROS AND SUGAR BOWL RESORT

In 1999, when my son Wildon was three and my daughter Emma was a year old, I decided to rein in the traveling aspect of my professional skiing career. Not that I gave it up completely. I still teach X-Team Advanced Ski Clinics in various locations in North and South America, Canada and Europe. But I also felt I wanted to develop another dimension to my career that would allow me to work closer to my home in Tahoe City, California. So I started All Mountain Ski Pros, my own ski instruction and guiding company based at Tahoe's Sugar Bowl Ski Resort.

I wasn't interest in assuming the traditional role of a professional ski instructor in America. I wanted to do my own thing. I really enjoy teaching and guiding people. I like the one-on-one aspect of helping people bring their skiing to the next level, helping them do things on skis they didn't think they could do. I like seeing people make breakthroughs and knowing that I had a part in it.

So I gathered a group of like-minded and talented ski pros (instructors and guides), who make skiing their lives, and trained them to teach all-mountain skiing using the teaching method that Rob and I developed, and which has been so successful. If you are interested in learning more about my company, and skiing or backcountry touring with me or one of my team, please contact me and I'll tell you all about it. I can be reached through allmountainskipros.com.

Sugar Bowl Ski Resort is the perfect location for All Mountain Ski Pros because it has a great variety of terrain within its boundaries, and an open-gate policy for the backcountry.

Sugar Bowl defines the term "powder stash." More and more people are skiing the Bowl, but they don't tell anyone about it. Right now it's a haven in the Tahoe area where fresh tracks can still be found—in-bounds—days after a storm and where you can ski a fantastic variety of terrain for all ability levels. At Sugar Bowl, we ski steeps that rival any other area with trees and open faces on a variety of terrain. It is the perfect place to ski the whole mountain.

Sugar Bowl has a modern lift system. Of the nine lifts, the four most important ones—those that access the best skiing—are all high-speed quads. Sugar Bowl boasts 1,500 acres of inbounds skiing with 84 trails. Thirty-eight percent of the mountain is advanced and another 45 percent of the terrain is intermediate-level cruising. Best of all, the area receives an average of 500 inches of snow every year.

Sugar Bowl is also nestled right smack in the middle of some of the best backcountry terrain in the northern Sierra, terrain that been used in ski and snowboard movies by Standard Films, Warren Miller, Scott Gaffney, and plenty of others. At Sugar Bowl we can ride the lift to the top of Mt. Lincoln and access the backcountry right from there, Chamonix style. So join us—we'll have a great time!

—Eric D.

The chutes at Sugar Bowl challenge the best of skiers. Here's Eric loving life on a nice steep one.

Check out Alzie (our good friend Allen Riley) ripping a groomer and making it look smooth and easy. He's perfectly aligned over his feet with a natural stance to hold his arc. Allen grew up with us at Bolton Valley, Vermont, where his parents, Steve and Deb, owned the Black Bear Lodge. Now he works with us on X-Team Clinics and for All Mountain Skis Pros.

chapter 1

ESSENTIALS OF ALL MOUNTAIN TECHNIQUE

Two-footed carving and the art of the simple transition.

Skiing well, skiing fast, skiing relaxed and strong is all about consistency and simplicity—and it all starts here, with your stance.

Your stance is simply your basic balanced body posture, the platform from which you'll make all the movements of good skiing. Good skiing means your body is constantly in motion as you flow from turn to turn. Your ideal stance mimics your body position when you are in transition between turns, when you are weightless and relaxed and both skis are flat to the snow surface. This is the point when you are flowing into your next turn and your skis are just coming onto edge.

This chapter outlines the foundation for the essential movements and techniques covered in the following chapters. You don't have to read it first. You can jump ahead to the specific chapters you are keenly interested in—like those on steeps or powder—and then return to this section for reference and several practice drills when you need to.

But, for many skiers, the key to improving your skiing is to accurately practice—on groomed runs—the essential movements outlined in this chapter. If you're out skiing the off-piste, and you find that you are always in survival mode, then you should read this chapter and practice these drills on groomed runs. It will be worth it. We promise.

The same core movements will soon have you skiing the whole mountain with grace and power. And the manicured runs provided by your favorite resorts offer the best arena to practice new skills. This controlled setting, with-out distractions like powder, bumps, and challenging terrain features is a perfect environment to really focus on executing the movements we are discussing and to experience the effortless and controlled feeling of the two-footed carve and the art of the simple transition.

Transition: The key to flow

From this point forward we will describe good skiing in terms of linking your turns from fall line to fall line. We won't talk about one turn at a time. The real magic of good skiing is in the transition from one turn to the next. Good skiing results when you link your turns. For many skiers, this will be a shift in focus, but it is critically important. To ski well it is absolutely key to focus on the completion of one turn, through the transition between turns, to the engagement of the skis in the next turn. Carve, release, transition, engage, carve—from the fall line of one turn to the fall line of the next.

Once you discover the sensations of linked, two-footed carved turns, you will look at yourself, and at other skiers, differently. You will also look back up the hill and think to yourself: "Did I just ski that? I'm not even tired and felt totally in control!" When you are executing these simple movements with total awareness, you will revel in the sensations coming from your skis. And you will be a much better skier.

A smooth transition from turn to turn requires consistent balance, which starts with a balanced stance. Try these exercises while just standing in one place. Then try them in a slow glide.

Eric in a chute at Squaw Valley. Notice the similarities between this photo of Eric and the one of Allen Riley on the previous page. The terrain is completely different, but the basic body geometry is the same.

From a good stance you should be able to roll both feet on edge at the same angles. If not, you may need to get your ski boots fitted and aligned correctly for how you stand. Make sure to get a qualified boot fitter to do this for you. With a proper stance you can lift your ski and set it back down to simulate the shock absorbing movement of your legs. Avoid having to slide your foot forward, then up. Instead, pick it straight up and then plunk it straight back down. Do not slide forward or back when making this movement.

You want to be able to do three basic things from a balanced, all-mountain stance:

1. Roll both skis on edge at the same angle. Play with the distance between your feet to get this just right. Each skier has a unique body shape, so experiment and find your ideal stance width. Keep your legs flexed and your upper body and arms poised for action. Think about the athletic "ready position" in other agility-based sports— soccer, football or baseball. When you're in a good stance, you should be able to tip both feet simultaneously and produce matching edge angles.

2. Lightly lift one foot and then the other with very little movement of the upper body. You will need to keep your legs nicely flexed to balance effectively.

3. Lift each ski until your thigh is parallel to the snow surface, then plunk it straight back down without ever losing shin to boot-tongue contact. Lift each foot directly upward, without having to slide it forward, then up. Keep your legs bent or flexed at all times; do not stand straight on either leg at any time. This stance exercise highlights the position of the legs relative to the hips and upper body. It facilitates the up and down movement of your legs to provide mid-turn shock absorbers and a flowing, strong and balanced transition into your next turn.

Take a look at Adam (our younger brother Adam DesLauriers) as he makes a short-radius steep turn in the Tioga Pass (California) backcountry. Notice the perfect setup of the hands, shoulders and eyes facing his next turn. Having just planted his pole with a light touch for timing, he is in perfect position for a balanced and relaxed transition into his next turn.

Upper body position

Your shoulders, hands and eyes all work together as one unit.

Shoulders: Your shoulders should be more or less over your toes and knees. This puts you in a strong balanced position to absorb terrain variations and to stand well on your skis at all times.

Hands: Keep your hands relatively low and out front, just at the edge of your peripheral vision. There's no magic hand position—just keep them comfortably in front, spread a bit apart for balance and stability.

Eyes: Keep your eyes focused on the middle of your next turn.

Summary: Your shoulders, hands and eyes work together and need to be aimed at the middle of your next turn. Keep in mind there is a difference between where your feet and skis will travel versus your eyes and shoulders. Your upper body will always be "inside" the arc of your carving skis, so that is where you want to be looking.

Fore-and-aft balance

With modern skis, there's no need for exaggerated fore/aft balancing adjustments, up-unweighting between turns, or conscious steering of the legs. The modern sidecuts and structural integrity of today's skis make it unnecessary, under most conditions, to actively apply pressure on the shovels of the skis to make them turn.

If you exert too much forward pressure, looking like an old school ski racer, you may overflex the shovels and buckle the ski or cause the skis to skid out of control. Or your turn may tighten more sharply than you anticipated, compromising balance and control. This can happen even on a groomed run, and especially at higher speeds.

Similarly, the old-fashioned powder stance (leaning back) is also unnecessary. It will drive your ski tails down into the snow (you'll be doing a "wheelie") which makes flowing in to the new turn very difficult to pull off.

This is a good angle to see how Rob's centered stance allows him to balance on his skis as he slices a medium-radius turn through silky-but-consolidated Grand Targhee powder. Note the vertical alignment of toes, knees and shoulders, with snug pressure of shins against boot tongues. From this stance he can easily carve with his weight on one foot or two, depending on speed and conditions.

This three-shot sequence shows that the simple focus on footwork creates balanced, linked turns. Notice especially the transition phase, from the release of one medium-radius turn to the engagement of the next. Photo I shows the finish of one turn with the left hand poised for a light pole plant. The edge angles are equal, and both skis are weighted. Photo 2 is just after the release of the turn, which is triggered by relaxing the outside foot and leg. You can actually see a shadow under the downhill ski, meaning that Eric's weight has transferred to his uphill (new outside ski). Notice how this simple, effortless lightening of the downhill ski draws his upper body downhill over his skis and towards the new turn. He focuses only on tipping the new inside foot lightly to its little-toe edge (Photo 3) which naturally arcs the skis and creates the perfect alignment of the body to carve the new turn.

With today's wide and shapely skis, these are now extraneous movements that can and should be eliminated. Skiing from a more centered stance, without a lot of forward or aft pressure, takes maximum advantage of your ski's design and makes great skiing easier in all conditions, with more control and less effort. Simple is better and way more versatile.

Two-footed carving

From a solid stance, great skiing is primarily about footwork. When your feet do the right things, balance comes naturally—you don't have to think about it.

With this in mind, let's look at skiing from the snow up. The technique is primarily about two-footed carving. It is about using both feet together (instead of one ski at a time) to create matching edge angles and to link your turns and carve sweet arcs in any snow conditions. The benefit of matching edge angles is that it makes your skis cut cleanly through the snow together, almost as one, for greater stability in varying snow conditions. If your edge angles are not matching to a significant degree, your skis are more likely to deflect in different directions, making control and efficiency harder to achieve in wide ranging snow conditions.

Two-footed carving does not mean that you will always have equal weight on both skis all the time. On the contrary, your weight on each ski will vary widely at different phases of the turn and in different snow and terrain conditions.

Medium-radius, groomer turn

Envision this: You are finishing a medium-sized turn, just coming out of the fall line. At this point, most of your weight is on your outside ski, especially if you're skiing firm snow. Your inside ski carries less weight but tracks parallel to the outside ski at a matching edge angle.

Here's where the footwork happens: As you are finishing your turn, plant your pole, then, to actively release your turn, take your weight off your outside leg by simply relaxing that foot and leg (Photo 1). This early weight transfer shifts your weight and balance to the uphill ski and triggers the natural edge change.

As your skis pass through neutral as in Photo 2 (when they go flat to the snow surface right underneath you), with your upper body facing your next turn, focus only on getting your new inside ski lightly onto its new turning edge (its little-toe side). Keeping the inside foot light (Photo 3) will actually center your balance and weight on your new outside foot. The ski bends and the turn starts. This whole movement sequence is the link between your turns. It's simple and seamless.

To summarize the turn-to-turn flow:

1. As your skis finish the turn, cutting across the fall line, release that turn (and the grip of your edges) by relaxing the outside leg.

2. This release triggers the natural transition and flow into the new turn. In this phase, you pass through neutral, relaxed and poised, and both skis go flat to the slope.

3. Engage the new turn by continuing to tip the light inside foot onto its little-toe side.

4. Congratulations: You have just linked balanced turns with less effort and more control.

Essentials in detail:

1. To experience the turn-to-turn flow more intensely, simultaneously relax and tip the outside foot and "shorten" this leg (by lifting your heel). This gets both skis quickly carving together into the new turn.

2. Focus on the tipping of the light inside foot. It is absolutely essential that you actively and consciously keep tipping that inside foot through the entire turn. Due to the matching edge angles that this movement creates, the turn radius and parallel tracking of the skis are consistent through each turn and you will be set up perfectly for your next transition (release, transfer, engage).

3. Your outside leg will match the edge angle that you establish with the inside foot and ski. It's a simple fact. Just focus on tipping your

TURN RADIUS

With modern skis, there's no need for exaggerated fore/aft balancing adjustments, up-unweighting between turns, or conscious steering or rotary movements of the legs. If you can tip (the skis on edge), you can rip.

The radius of your turn is controlled mainly by how quickly you move your feet from turn to turn, how quickly you put the skis on edge and how high you tip the skis on edge. Turn your skis up quickly to a high edge angle—and you'll get a short-radius turn. Roll the skis up on edge more unhurriedly—and you'll get a long-radius turn.

light, inside foot on edge while maintaining a balanced and properly targeted upper body, and you will be carving like never before.

Old habits

As you begin to understand these simplified movements, it's also important to understand what movements will inhibit success—movements that you must unlearn if they are ingrained habits.

First among these "undesirable moves" is the classic stem, including the stem christie. To transition from one turn to the next, you step from the inside (big-toe) edge of the downhill ski to the inside (big-toe) edge of the new outside ski. This can make the start of the turn easier, and it works well enough at slow speeds on groomed or smooth snow. But in deep, soft snow it doesn't work.

A second movement to avoid is parallel skidding—twisting or oversteering of the ski through the top of each turn and into the fall line. This has been taught in many ski schools as the parallel christie. Imagine trying to skid your skis sideways through deep snow to start every turn. It's only a matter of time before you'd get tripped up or collapse in an exhausted heap.

To replace the stem or the skid, you need to learn two-footed carving.

Two-footed carving

What follows is a step-by-step progression to help you learn two-footed carving. Special notes are included for stemmers and skidders so that you'll know where extra practice is needed to unlearn those habits. The progression includes three drills that will lead to groomed snow carving, then a fourth carved-turn drill putting it all together on groomed snow. After mastering the fourth drill, you can jump into carving powder and crud and everything else. The drills are:

- the javelin
- traverse on the little-toe edge
- the "I-can't-believe-it's-so-easy-to-turn" drill
- carves on the groomed

Over the past few ski seasons, these simple exercises have proven to be the most effective to introduce the aspiring all-mountain skiers to a new understanding of the footwork to achieve the balanced carve turns we are after. This holds true for almost all ability levels, from very low intermediates to full-on expert skiers. Give it a go and enjoy.

Remember: Drills exaggerate reality to emphasize a point. All these drills are executed entirely on one foot at a time, focusing on balance and the essential movements. If you can perform these drills properly and in balance throughout, you will be on you way to ripping carves in all conditions.

t

nto
th
ins You'll
fin th
har ance.)
or the
com (Fig. 2).

Essen ki by
pivoting his will
only lead eslip.
Instead, yo tipped on
edge and car nstrated
by Rob in Fig

2: Traverse on little-toe edge (uphill ski)

This drill will help you discover the feeling of standing on the little-toe edge of your uphill ski and leg at the end of each turn. You will actually glide on the uphill edge of your uphill ski all the way across the hill. For those who stem or skid into each turn, this will be a critical new sensation, one that's absolutely essential for fluid carving from turn to turn.

We cannot emphasize enough how critical the use of this uphill edge is in all-mountain skiing. It separates the intermediate from the expert. You need to do this drill until you can perform it in balance all the way across the hill and consciously experience the sensation of riding this edge.

The drill is simple to explain, but it's not always easy to perform right away. Be patient and learn to do this in balance.

Simply traverse across a wide slope on the uphill (little-toe) edge of your uphill ski (Fig. I). Notice that the downhill ski stays completely off the snow, forcing you to balance on that uphill edge.

Move your hips slightly uphill to put weight directly over the uphill ski, and make sure that your uphill ski is slightly ahead of your downhill ski. This will "open" the hips a touch, making them face slightly down the hill—a perfect position from which to start a new turn.

Essentials: Traverse first in one direction, then in the other, and don't do a sliding traverse—carve the ski cleanly into the snow across the hill. You may find yourself actually carving back up the hill on that little-toe edge.

3: The I-can't-believe-it's-so-easy-to-turn-drill

This is a fantastic drill. It will help you experience the flow of linked carved turns. It is an extension of the uphill-edge traverse drill described above and flows (literally) into the javelin drill. Success in this drill eradicates stemming and skidding in turn initiation. It hones the all-mountain turn transition we've been discussing and is the key to all-terrain versatility. For many it will be your first experience with a complete carved turn.

While gliding across the hill on the uphill edge of your uphill ski (exactly as you did in drill #2), simply tip your unweighted or lifted inside ski (of your upcoming turn) down the hill into that new turn (Fig. 1).

Notice how this simple tipping action moves Rob's upper body nicely downhill to the inside of the turn. This action also has the effect of engaging the big-toe edge of your weighted ski, which is your dominant turning ski (Fig. 2).

Wa-boom! You have just carved the top of the turn, a skill formerly limited to experts only.

To complete the carve, simply balance mostly on that outside ski, mimicking the one-footed carving sensation of the javelin drill.

Essentials: You can actually use the inside ski for balance if you just keep it lightly brushing the snow surface.

4: Carves on the groomed

In Figs. 1-2, Eric rips up a groomed trail with both skis tipped on edge and the inside ski just lightly brushing the snow. At this point in the turn, you have any combination of weighting between your feet.

In Figs. 2-3, he releases the turn and transfers more weight to his uphill ski (future outside leg) by shortening his current outside leg (exactly as in Drill 2).

By Fig. 4, he has completed the weight transfer and initiated his new turn by tipping the recently unweighted ski to the inside of the turn (exactly as in Drill 3).

By Fig. 5-6 the forces are building on the outside ski, bending it into the arc. The inside ski is poised ready to carry weight as needed to carve the turn on two skis and be there for the next release and transition.

Essentials: Notice how Eric never comes up, or rises, between turns. He is solid in every phase of the turn. He can take these exact movements into the un-groomed, all-mountain realm.

The combination of drills 1, 2 and 3 will enable you to carve the top of your new turn directly from your previous turn, eliminating that shaky moment between turns when many skiers hesitate. This is the key to slicing through crud.

For those who are used to stemming or skidding, this movement will seem foreign or awkward because there is little or no upward projecting of the body, or stemming or skidding of the skis. You'll simply tip your feet from one side (completing turn) to the other side (new turn). Practice this until you find your balance.

Welcome to the world of all-mountain skiing. Build these moves into your skiing and you'll be skiing the whole mountain faster, smoother, more in control and with a lot less effort then you're used to. Believe it.

Role of the upper body

As soon as you can perform the footwork described above in good balance, you can basically quit worrying about your upper body. It has to be doing the right thing. Your upper body is a key element of sound skiing and plays a critical role. However, it is not the first issue you need to address. Footwork is the primary concern, so work on that first. If you feel as if you are getting the footwork right, but are still not in balance, or are skidding, or losing control on steeps, or not feeling confident in linking your turns—then your upper body position may need refinement.

It is a popular misconception that your shoulders and hands should be facing straight down the hill all the time. Many ski instructors have taught this technique, which produces a twisting of the waist they call "counter rotation." The new skis, with their deep sidecuts, make it so much easier to start a new turn that we can now greatly simplify the upper body position. We need much less counter rotation than previously thought.

The new, relaxed and balanced stance involves a very natural upper body position. You want your hands, shoulders and eyes pointing right to the middle of your next turn.

In a tight fall line turn, your shoulders and eyes face aggressively down the fall line, because that is where you are going.

In a long-radius, super-G turn, your shoulders and eyes face more across the slope as you are finishing your turn (towards the middle of your next turn), because that's where you are headed.

The slight counter rotation at the end of your turn provides all the rotary energy you need to help draw your skis into your next turn as your

With a nasty-looking Vermont-style crux move staring him in the face, Adam's shoulders, hands and eyes are focused on where he wants to go, and he's ready for a quick transition into his new turn.

A high speed, long-radius cruiser at Grand Targhee. In Photo I, Eric is just coming through the fall line, focused on his next turn. Notice how extended his legs are in this shot. Both skis are carving. By Photo 2, he has already started to release this turn by slowly relaxing the outside leg, and the outside leg has gotten shorter. He continues this releasing movement by relaxing his outside foot and leg in Photo 3, where both skis are flat to the snow surface. Even though the speed is fast, the footwork is relatively slow because he started the move up in the arc.

skis are swinging under you and rolling onto the new edge. When the edge change is done accurately, you should have no need for twisting or actively steering your skis into your turn. This simplifies your movement, because you can focus entirely on the tipping movements of your feet to create the turn. Simple is good.

Higher-speed arcs

In high-speed, long-radius turns, the action of releasing the turn occurs slower than when you are linking short, snappy turns. The challenge is to stay focused and move your feet at a rate consistent with your turn radius. In other words, in a long-radius turn, you do not want to just snap your skis onto the new turning edges. You want a longer transition with a slower edge change. It's not a question of how quickly you change edges, but rather how truly.

When you release a high-speed ripper by relaxing the outside leg, balance is transferred to the uphill foot. As the transfer of weight progresses, you will quickly have equal weight on both skis, with both legs bent and relaxed. At this point, continue to slowly shorten and lighten the downhill leg to complete the weight transfer to the uphill (new outside) ski. Then, by laying the new inside ski lightly on its turning edge (little-toe edge), you'll automatically engage the turning edge of the new outside ski, thereby creating another carved turn. Again, have patience as you allow the skis to carve through the new turn.

Let's move on and jet around the world a bit. In the next few chapters, we'll look at this simple two-footed carve in a variety of snow conditions, on different mountains and on four continents.

Pack your skis and let's go.

STANCE TECH TALK

Off-piste skiing is easier and more fun when you use two-footed carving, with both skis working together, carving the same arc all the way through the turn. For that, both skis need to be at pretty much equal edge angles to the snow.

Your stance width plays a big role in this. Some people can create equal edge angles with their feet wide apart. But not many. For most people, a wide stance (say, greater then your shoulder-width apart) creates an "A-frame" effect in which the inside edges oppose each other. When this happens to inexperienced skiers, they usually cross their tips. When the skis are too far apart, it's also very easy to overload the weighted, outside ski. In deep snow, this can lead to burying it. With one ski deep in the powder and the other one arcing for the other side of the mountain, you can expect trouble.

The reverse is also true. When the feet are too close

COURTESY OF SKI MAGAZINE ARCHIVES

Even in the 1950s and '60s, the best skiers tipped their skis on edge at equal angles, with the inside foot tipping aggressively to the little-toe side. The skier: Legendary Austrian World Cup champion Karl Schranz, shown here racing at Wengen, Switzerland, in 1965. Note the deep bend in his outside ski.

together, the skis tend to oppose each other and therefore will not match edge angles. More important, the weighted, dominant ski can't achieve a high enough edge angle, so you get a less powerful carve and a oftentimes a skidded turn. This could be why skiers who emulate the locked-together Stein Eriksen style look really good in bumps and nowhere else, and why they often look as if they are skidding. They can't make both skis carve together, so they have to skid. Only Stein can carve like Stein!

With a more narrow or neutral stance in which your skis are about hip-width apart, and with matching edge angles, it's easy to flow your turns together in a wide variety of snow conditions. You're less likely to cross your tips, skid your turns or bury a ski in deep snow. But to achieve this you need both skis working together—all the time.

Here it is: All the essentials of all-mountain technique, applied to the steeps. Notice the eyes and hands and shoulders facing the new turn, the new inside foot tipping into the new turn and leading the edge change for the new outside ski.

Yeah, baby! There is simply nothing better in skiing than fine, light bottomless powder snow. All that's required is a bit of confidence and patience. Location: Squaw Valley off Red Dog Ridge. Skier: Eric.

chapter 2

POWDER SNOW

It's not that hard, and the rewards are incredible.

Powder snow is every skier's dream. We all know—or have heard—that flying through untracked powder is the most fun you can have on skis, period.

Why? There's a sense of weightless freedom, of speed and exhilaration. When powder is fresh and consistent, there's smoothness—the sense that you don't have to slow down to compensate for changing conditions. When you have the technique and the rhythm for it, there's a feeling that powder makes your turns for you. Powder feels elemental—it almost takes the equipment out of the performance equation. To an accomplished powder hound, it often feels as if you could ski the stuff on oak floorboards.

At the same time that we revere the glorious cold light white, we must acknowledge that your first excursion into deep snow can be a torturous, exhausting experience. If you ski a hard-snow technique—outside ski to outside ski, never really using both feet together—then you will struggle. If you overturn, twisting your skis against the snow, you may not even last to lunchtime before fatigue drives you back to the groomed runs, exhausted and sweating.

Happily, it doesn't take long to learn a simple, efficient technique that will work in any kind of powder snow.

Types of powder

The Eskimos have about 100 words to describe different types of snow. There are a lot of different types of powder snow. However, for purposes of ski technique, we can boil these down to four.

First, there is fluffy powder over a packed-snow base. In this type of powder, your skis contact the solid base as you finish each turn. This is what you commonly get the morning after a storm in-bounds at a ski resort.

Second, there is the much-sought-after dry and deep bottomless pow, where you feel like you're floating effortlessly through space, and the powder blows over your head so that you feel you can't breathe. It's so dry you plow right through it, and it's so deep your skis never reach bottom. This low-water-content kind of powder is found mostly in the backcountry or on runs accessed by helicopter or snowcat operations.

Third, there is heavy, higher-water-content powder. Most skiers don't go paying the big bucks for this type, but it can be fun, too, if you know how to ski it. Once you get the rhythm, your skis will go in and out of the snow providing really fun sensations.

Finally, there's wind-packed or variable powder. This is loose snow packed by the wind or by other factors, like temperature swings. If it is more loose than packed, it can still classify as powder. But when someone brags about skiing wind-packed powder all day, you may want to ask if he or she is headed back tomorrow for more of the same.

Use the right tools

If you're an intermediate skier and new to powder, start by finding a pair of fat skis—85mm at the waist or wider. Fat skis definitely help the uninitiated skier not only survive but have fun. The fat ski provides a wide platform, so it rides

Who says you never ski powder in Vermont? We both learned to ski powder right here growing up. It's not bottomless fluff, but it's still a blast! It's a slower rhythm than on packed snow, but the all-mountain technique is the same. Dean Decas shows how it's done in Devil's Playground at Bolton Valley Ski Area.

Left: Rob in quintessential deep powder in Chamonix. There's nothing hard in this photo except for the rocks. Above: A rooster-tail of light powder. Notice in all these photos that the hands, at the end of each turn, are reaching down the hill for the next pole plant. This helps to get your rhythm and keeps the upper body centered for a smooth, patient release.

high, close to the snow surface. When your skis float near the surface instead of diving deep into the snowpack, you can get away with marginal powder-skiing technique. If you have to steer and skid from time to time or end up with too much weight on one foot, fat skis allow you to do so without consequence.

If you're an advanced skier, wide-body or mid-fat skis—75mm to 85mm at the waist—provide the ultimate deep powder experience, while linking the smoothest turns you could ever dream up. With this wider ski, you can ski faster, make longer radius turns with ease and do things that are almost impossible on traditional-width (64mm to 68mm) skis. The wider ski lets you easily vary your turn radius to suit your style and the shape of the mountain. It encourages super-G turns in waist-deep powder, with simple,

consistent moves—something only snowboarders could do before wider skis became available.

Traditional or racing-width skis can work in powder. We learned to ski powder on traditional skis. But they are somewhat limiting, because the skis want to go deep into the snow on every turn. It's a great experience—who doesn't like the fabled powder snow face shots? But you can't go as fast, and you can't crank long turns the way you can on wider skis. Traditional skis force you to ski with a much more pronounced porpoising action, altering your stance and applying varying degrees of fore-aft and foot-to-foot weight shifts throughout each turn.

Not so with the new mid-fat and fat skis. Surface area is everything for powder skiing and, basically, one fat ski equals two skinny skis. You do the math.

Remember that photo on the first page of Chapter I of Allen Riley laying down nice arcs on a groomed run? Here's Rob at Grand Targhee skiing knee-deep powder with exactly the same body position at the finish of the turn. With modern wide skis, the movement is so similar, everyone can progress from groomed runs to powder.

Rhythm changes

With wider skis, you can ski powder with the same fundamental, two-footed technique you developed on groomed runs. You will, in fact, carve the powder.

However, the rhythm of powder skiing is slower than the rhythm on hard snow. We're not talking about slower speed but about a slower movement of the feet and legs to link your turns. On a firm surface, the skis and feet roll from turn to turn. In powder, with no firm surface to react against, the skis and the feet float from turn to turn, albeit with the same all-mountain footwork and edge changes. They do that, of course, when you create a good two-ski platform for balance, flotation and control.

Chamonix, France, with the Dru (a classic 1,000-meter rock climb) in the background. Check out the skinny little tips. It's not all about fat skis. See how the inside foot is tipping into the turn and actually sets the edge for the outside ski. Patience is the key. Move your feet slower then you think you should, focus on making a long transition, then tighten your turn as your skis sink in to the snow in your next turn.

Here's Eric looking downhill at all the possibilities for a lot of really nice turns. Looking down the hill gives you perspective and helps you link your turns. Location: Craigieburn, New Zealand.

Stance revisited

Your stance should be fundamentally the same as the one you practiced on groomed snow.

- Knees over your toes
- Legs flexed
- Shoulders balanced over the feet
- You may find that staying a little lower, with your legs flexed a bit more deeply, can provide better stability.

Fore-and-aft stance

Most of the time you want to stay centered, with your weight balanced equally over toes and heels, while maintaining slight shin pressure against your boot tongues. But different speeds require small adjustments.

In low-speed powder turns, you want to put a little more weight on your heels, with your toes lifted up to keep your boots snug to your shins.

When you are warping long-radius big-mountain turns in powder, you want to have a slightly more forward stance. This stance provides the right blend of finesse with strength and power to pull off a Mach 5 powder turn. You definitely do not want to overpower the front of the skis, though.

Stay low in the transition phase of your turn for better balance. The lower stance also facilitates the retraction of your legs in transition. This allows you to adapt more efficiently to terrain and snow changes and smooths the flow of your feet into the new turn.

CRAIGIEBURN, NEW ZEALAND

Some years ago we had an incredible two weeks in Craigieburn, New Zealand, a small "club field" (it's owned and operated by a ski club) about two hours south of Christchurch on the South Island.

This place is a true skiers' area, with three "nutcracker" rope tows that haul you an incredible 1,800 vertical feet up into two huge powder bowls. The vast steep terrain is a match for Jackson Hole or Squaw Valley—but it never sees more than 60 people at a time on the whole mountain!

The family-style operation offers half-a-dozen private cabins and a small lodge, where everyone helps with the cooking and dishes.

We spent our first week completely snowed in, climbing the walls of a small cabin on the far side of the base area. At one point photographer Hank deVre narrowly missed being buried in an avalanche as he was heading for the cabin.

When the storm passed, it left three or four feet of fresh, light powder. The club opened the tows that evening and invited us to join them. We helped dig out the top tow, then went powder skiing under a full moon. The good weather held for the following week, and we shot all the pics you see here.

If you go, watch out for the keas. These mountain parrots are the national bird of New Zealand. They're cute, but they're really bold thieves and vandals. At the ski area, they'll eat the rubber grips off your poles and tear your backpack to shreds. If you shoot them, you're in for a $30,000 fine.

Above: The Cabin.
Left: A hardcore Club Member heading up for more freshies on the high speed lift. Notice the fat skis.

This two-shot sequence of Eric at Valle Nevado, Chile, really shows how the footwork in the transition draws the upper body naturally into the new turn. Photo 1 shows how to release the turn with a pole plant and by relaxing the outside foot. You can see the upper body is still uphill of the skis. What you can't see is that it is already moving over the skis. Focus on relaxing and then tipping the new inside foot to start a chain reaction that draws the upper body across the skis into the new turn (Photo 2) with no effort at all.

The powder transition

In powder the rhythm is slower than on packed slopes, which means that the transition between turns takes longer. In fact, in powder, you cover more vertical distance during the transition phase of the turn than you do on firm snow. Here's the powder transition sequence:

Start your release early in each turn (just as your skis start to cut across the slope) by relaxing your outside foot even when both feet are equally weighted (Photo 1).

Weighting both feet equally creates a wider platform to finish each turn closer to the snow surface. This makes it more like skiing a groomed run and therefore makes it easier to ski well. We will discuss this in more detail later in the chapter.

Have patience in the transition to allow both skis to cut through and float out of the deep, powder snow as you slowly tip your inside foot into the new turn.

Then, as your skis continue to surface and you pass through neutral, keep tipping your inside foot which leads both skis onto the new turning edges (Photo 2).

It is a slow, rhythmic move. The new turn starts as the skis are skimming the snow surface and just coming onto the new turning edges.

Don't be afraid to roll your feet more slowly than you're used to doing. Your speed control comes not from a quick, early edge-change, but

THE GREEK RECOVERY

Check out Dean Decas in this photo sequence. The "Greek" (so named because he is Greek) is the originator of the fashionable goggles-on-the-forehead look. This works really great in lift lines, not so well when skiing bottomless powder.

In Photo 1, Dean can't see a thing except the inside of his shades.

In Photo 2, he pops out of the pow and sees the big 'ol rock he is about to plow into.

In Photo 3, to avoid imminent disaster, Dean lifts his skis and sets them in the new turn (none too soon). Lift and place! Photo 4. Notice the goggles on the forehead.

Timing is key: You need to lift the skis when you have the skis loaded and flexed. If you wait too long, the skis will unload and you won't be able to take advantage of their stored energy. You'll then have to muscle the skis out of the snow. Practice retracting the legs as early as possible. Then place the redirected skis into the next turn to make it happen quickly.

from the shape of your turn. Because your skis float smoothly at the beginning of the turn, most of the direction change and speed control happens as the turn tightens toward its end—as you pass through the fall line and beyond. Use a long transition to connect the turns, and tighten the turn as you finish the turn across the hill. The more you finish your turn (the more you get your skis pointing across the slope at the end of each turn), the more you slow down. However, it is often the case that overturning or getting the skis pointing too far across the slope and slowing down too much ruins the smooth flow.

By controlling your speed with turn shape, you can ski down the slope at whatever consistent speed you are comfortable with, making the same essential movements you were making on the groomed trails.

The essential points:

Relax your feet and legs to release the turn while keeping your upper body facing your next turn.

Transition from turn to turn by patiently leading the edge change with the new inside foot tipping to its new turning edge. This will ensure that both skis enter each turn in parallel and at matching edge angles.

Have patience as the skis near the surface. Patience is important because you have to allow your skis to surface, to unweight, before rolling onto the new turning edges. If you are impatient and do not allow your skis to surface, you will struggle with your skis under the snow as we described earlier in this chapter.

Make bigger turns than you think you should.

TECH TALK: ROTARY MOTION

The photo on the facing page shows that Eric's eyes and shoulders are directed right toward the middle of the next turn. The skis are skimming the surface of the snow, floating effortlessly into the new turn.

Because the shoulders are facing the middle of the turn while the skis are still pointing across the hill, Eric's midsection is twisted. There's a rotary force, or torque, building between the upper body and the legs. This counter rotation between the heavier upper body and the much lighter lower body will help your skis seek the fall line during the transition between turns. That's because when you release your edges at the end of the turn, your body wants to realign itself or untwist. When you release your turn and your skis pass through neutral, the uncoiling of your midsection will help the skis seek the fall line—you won't even have to think about it. Orienting your shoulders and chest toward the middle of the next turn therefore simplifies your movement, because all you need to think about is laying your skis on edge.

With good upper body positioning at the end of each turn, you can focus purely on the lateral edging of the skis. Lead the edge change with the new inside foot, have patience and let your skis seek the fall line on their own.

Medium-radius powder turn

Let's take a look at the medium-radius turn, because this is the most natural turn in powder. The modern ski loves this turn radius when tipped up on edge. With the appropriate mid-fat ski, this turn can feel very relaxed and basically effortless.

In the next sequence, shot at Squaw Valley, California, the snow is glory powder about three feet deep, on a slope of about 35 degrees. It's a perfect pitch for this cold, superlight snow, which has a moisture content of only about six percent. This snow is so light that the rooster tail behind the average skier stretches about 40 feet long and 10 feet high.

Remember the premise of this book: The same core movements work for all types of skiing and snow conditions. It is a way of moving that, when programmed into your style, will provide powerful turns with less effort and more control, so you can ski the whole mountain with poise and confidence.

In the photo on the facing page, Eric passes through what we call the pure neutral moment in the turn.

Both skis are flat to the snow and he's totally weightless and relaxed.

Lead the edge change with the inside foot to achieve matching edge angles to enter the new turn. Both feet are pulled up (or retracted) and angled together so you are perfectly poised to enter the new turn.

Although this posture may look as if the skier is leaning back, that is an illusion. The stance is actually centered perfectly for the deep snow.

The shins are snug against the tongues of the boots. This is totally key. You want to maintain snug contact between your shins and the tongues of your ski boots.

There is no need to consciously steer your skis by twisting your feet. Deep snow resists any steering action, so if you try to twist your skis into the turn, you'll often exert far too much unnecessary effort and probably catch an edge and do a head plant. Inherently, there is rotary movement in all good skiing. However, with modern skis, there is no need to make this an active, conscious movement. The upper body

Pure neutral. Notice how the skis are leading the way out of the previous turn. They are coming straight out of the snow with no twisting movements. You can see that the inside ski is slightly higher than the uphill ski. This shows that the inside ski is actively moving and leading the movement of the uphill foot (soon to be the outside foot). Skier: Eric in Silverado Bowl, Squaw Valley.

Photo 1 shows the very top of the turn, with both skis working together and already cutting the snow and shaping the new turn. Eric's weight is just starting to settle on the skis to further bend them into the turn. Never get anxious here and overturn the skis or drive them too quickly down into the snow. Patience, patience, patience. In Photo 2, Eric's weight is settling naturally onto his skis, driving them deeper into the snow as the turn comes around and edge angle increases to tighten the turn (providing speed control).

positioning described in the sidebar on the previous page will provide all the force needed to draw the skis into the fall line. Instead of steering your skis, focus only on tipping the skis on edge, with the inside foot light. Keep it simple.

The rock-solid stance in photo 1 provides the perfect blend of power and finesse to carve the skis through the powder. The turning of the skis towards the fall line has already started as a result of a well positioned upper body. Notice how quiet and stable the upper body is.

At this point, the shape of modern skis and the resistance offered by the deep snow bends the skis into the arc of the turn with very little extra pressure exerted by the skier. Even in light powder, by the time the skis are laid on edge at the top of the turn—even before your weight settles onto them—they start coming around into the new turn. Then, as the skis actually sink into the snow, they bend even more, creating the turn without any fore-aft movement by the skier. On old-style straight skis, you would need to actively pressure first the front and then the rear of the skis to get them to turn and then resurface to link your turns. With modern skis, your good stance and simple technique will power the skis through

In Photo 3, Eric's skis are just about to "bottom out" in the powder. Both skis are equally weighted. Check out the curl of snow from both skis. Very cool. The left hand is reaching for a pole plant. Photo 4 is the beginning of the rebound up through the snow, just after the pole plant. Remember: Don't wait too long and finish your turn too much or you'll lose that rebound effect.

the snow and then provide an effortless transition to link all your turns.

Of course, the wider the skis, the less they will sink into the snow. More surface area means more float, making the whole process of smooth powder skiing much easier. On super-fats, even shallow, fresh powder can feel silkier than the smoothest groomed run you've ever skied.

In photos 2-3, the G's are building as the turn continues, and Eric's body settles onto the skis, forcing them down into the snow. This is the beginning of the "control" part of turn, where you settle onto the skis. You settle into a low, strong stance and ride through the turn. With the good balance you create, you can choose to ride a long turn or a short one. Once you are in the pocket and riding through the turn, you can hold the arc anywhere from a split second in a tight, speed-control turn to several seconds in a long, fast turn. In either case, a good stance provides the base for you to track cleanly in the deep snow.

In photo 4 you can just see the tips coming back to the surface, because Eric is slowly relaxing both legs together and gently pulling his feet and toes up. With good timing on this release move, the skis and natural forces mentioned above provide the energy needed to rise to the surface. The trick is to trigger the release of the turn while you are still in the turn, meaning the skis are still flexed like a loaded trampoline.

This is Photo 5 of the sequence. You can see the active movement of the new inside foot coming out the turn. Both feet have come up and the new inside foot is leading the edge change (with a somewhat exaggerated lifting move). If you can get to this point in the transition with your skis flat to the hill and skimming the snow surface, you are perfectly poised to make your next turn a good one.

TECH TALK: THE LAST WORD ON POWDER

The real trick in powder snow is that you need to have both skis exit one turn and enter the next, in parallel, with no steering.

On groomed snow, you can get away with twisting of the skis and other extraneous moves, because the smooth surface allows for mistakes and recoveries. In powder, your skis have to carve forward, through the snow. You need precision to cut the snow cleanly.

What holds the skis in an arc is the pressure of the snowpack against the bases of your edged skis. At the bottom of the turn, the skis track across the hill the way a water ski cuts across the wake. It often feels as if the snow is pushing back.

So, when you release a turn by relaxing your legs, your skis rebound off the pressure of the snow. The released energy helps to float the skis closer to the snow surface. There they'll pass through the neutral phase of the turn as they skim the surface and flow into the new turn.

If you wait too long to transition into the new turn and go into a traverse, the skis will straighten out and you will lose this inherent energy. Without the trampoline effect from your muscles and your flexed skis, you'll be forced to "double clutch" and throw the skis into the new turn. However, with good timing to release the energy of the turn, you can simply relax both legs to trigger the rise of the skis and the retraction of your legs and skis. As soon as the skis rise up, initiate your edge change by tipping your new inside foot. Now you're back to the neutral phase of the transition, with the skis flat to the snow surface.

This continous move should be done at a rate consistent with the turn radius you are making. In this medium-radius sequence, on mid-fats, it is a surprisingly slow move—a one-two count to bring the skis to the surface.

As the skis skim the surface, you want to continue tipping the inside ski to its new turning edge in the rhythm you have already established. This is the point in the turn when you really do not want to twist or steer you skis.

Once again, the technique for skiing untracked powder on modern shaped skis, especially on wider skis, is fundamentally the same as for skiing groomed runs. Your core movements are:

- the release
- the transfer of weight to the uphill ski
- the transition from one set of edges to the new set of edges as the skis travel from one side of your body to the other)
- the engagement of the new turn.

The good news is that the powder itself, when you have the rhythm and technique down pat, will actually help you to make the turns. Powder skiing becomes effortless when you get the touch.

Short-radius powder turn

The short-radius powder turn is particularly useful in tight trees and chutes. You'll use basically the same technique with all types of skis. We shot these pictures in Craigieburn, New Zealand. The snow is about three feet deep and Rob is making short-radius turns at a moderate speed. For this type of turn in deep powder, there is a little bit of fore-aft balancing to be done, even on a wide ski. You want to create a little heel pressure to finish each turn, then regain your centered stance as you flow through neutral into the next turn. As you

POWDER TRICKS OF THE MASTERS

Here are a few powder skiing tricks to help you handle adverse conditions:

To slow down in the middle of your turn, just lean slightly forward to go deeper into the snow. Pressure the front of your skis—that will push them deeper into the snow and slow you down almost immediately. This is handy if you're surprised by something unexpected and you need to hit the brakes.

Overextended outside leg? Sometimes an unexpected drop-off or patch of lighter snow "collapses" under your outside (dominant) ski. Maybe you're moving at mach speed, and the outside ski simply breaks away. To recover your balance in midturn, just retract or shorten that outside leg. This action shifts your balance onto the inside/uphill ski, which you can ride long enough to recover your balance.

Deep powder making you tired? Try making longer turns. It is less effort, very efficient and lots of fun!

To change direction quickly—in effect, to change direction in midturn—quickly retract your legs to create a transition and set them down in the direction of the new turn. This takes good timing, but it helps you to turn on a dime and is a great recovery move when you need it. See The Greek Recovery.

Above: Smile and release your turn early before your skis point all the way across the hill. **Right:** It just doesn't get any better then this. Rob in deep at Grand Targhee.

New Zealand's Alps are larger in mass than the European Alps. Dean Decas loving life at Craigieburn.

It's just easier on wide skis. This sequence of Rob was shot on skinny (traditional) skis, however the movements are the same as on wide skis. Rob is releasing this turn just as his skis bottom out and hit the firmer snow under the soft fluff. Photo 2 shows the middle of the new turn with the skis driving into the snow for speed control. This happens by applying a tad more forward pressure as the skis come into the fall line.

engage the new turn, use a little forward pressure to push the skis down into the snow, thus shaping your turn to control your speed.

Because this is a short-radius turn, the rhythm is quicker than in the medium-radius turn. Release the pressure at the end of the turn by relaxing the outside leg and immediately tip this same foot to its little toe edge.

You can see in photo 1 that Rob's upper body is set a bit back from vertical above his feet and knees. Although his shins are still snug against his boot tongues, he is pressuring his heels. The heel pressure on the skis, combined with this upper body position, will push the tails of the skis deeper into the snow and keep his ski tips riding up close to the surface. From here he can release his turn by relaxing his outside foot and then retracting both feet together. Right away, he tips his new inside ski to lead the edge change into the new turn. This will create a natural porpoising motion of the skis, into and out of the snow as he flows through neutral and into the new turn.

It is also really important at this point to reach with your pole plant down the fall line toward your next turn, to help your upper body flow into the new turn.

Photo 2 shows the middle of the next turn. Because this is a tight spot, Rob cannot stretch this turn out too much. He is forced to make a relatively slow-speed, tight turn to get through this notch in the terrain. He is coming

Exiting the turn. The key to linking these turns is to avoid finishing your turn too far forward on the skis and losing your momentum. If you get too far forward, your skis will dive to the bottom like a depth charge. You will more than likely slow down too much and lose your rhythm or take a header over the bars.

into this turn leading the edge change with the light inside foot. The more you can actively tip the skis to a maximum edge angle at this point, the more it will help to create a shorter radius and effectively shape the top of this turn.

Then, as he settles onto the skis, he is well into the middle of the turn. He is pressuring slightly forward to actively push both skis deeper into the snow—this controls his speed. He pressures both skis together, with a subtle down movement, to create the two ski platform (see sidebar, Creating the Two Ski Platform).

Then (photo 3), as Rob hits bottom and begins to rebound upward, he relaxes the downhill foot and retracts both legs. As always, he leads the edge change with the new inside ski tipping to its little-toe edge. He is now perfectly poised to flow into the new turn.

The long-radius powder turn is the greatest beneficiary of wide skis. Making long-radius turns in powder will change your perspective on what it means to ski the whole mountain.

Long-radius powder turn

The long-radius powder turn is the greatest advance in skiing technique to come out of the modern wide-ski evolution. With wider skis, the long-radius high-speed turn uses almost exactly the same movement pattern as in long-radius turns on groomed snow. The turn provides a really smooth, powerful and fun ride. The build-up and release of forces is effortless and smooth as silk.

This type of turn was barely possible on traditional-width skis, because at higher speeds the G-forces simply buried the skis in the deep snow. When the skis go that deep, you spend all your time trying to balance against their deceleration. Most of time, even good skiers who pick up a lot of speed on narrow skis will usually end up slowing down or dropping into a figure 11—that is, a straight run down the hill.

Photo 1 shows the midpoint of the turn, as the skis are just coming out of the fall line. Eric's weight is settling onto the skis. The G

forces have started to build, and the natural forces have caused the skis to sink into the snow. Eric has matched the edge angles of his skis and is ready to create a solid two-ski platform. His stance is low and centered.

In photo 2 you can see more snow flying, so you know that the skis are going deeper into the snow. Body position is low, powering the skis through the snow. This is a good body position. You can see that, as the pressure increases on the skis, the upper body centers forward over the feet—poised to power through the bottom of the turn.

Eric continues the ride through the turn, still loading both skis. This does not really mean it is a 50/50 weight distribution between the skis. It can be 70 percent on the outside ski and 30 percent on the inside ski, or it could be 60/40, or even 80/20. Go with whatever works at the time and feels good. When we skied on narrow, 65mm giant slalom skis, we needed a 50/50 weight distribution to avoid burying the outside ski. Today,

The views and alpenglow sunsets we've seen at Valle Nevado, Chile, rival those we've seen anywhere in the world. Larry Segal airs it out on a summit ridge off the high-speed Andes Express quad lift.

VALLE NEVADO, CHILE

Valle Nevado (vah-yay nehVAHdo) is the largest and most modern ski resort in South America. Nine lifts cover an incredible 24,000 acres of great skiing (just for comparison, the biggest area in North America, Whistler/Blackcomb, covers 7,000 acres). By upgrading to the full valley ticket, you can also ski neighboring resorts La Parva and El Colorado, which doubles the available skiing terrain.

Originally developed by a French company, Valle Nevado has four cool-looking modern hotels, plus seven restaurants, a crazy discothèque that doesn't even heat up until 1:00 a.m., and a huge round tub filled with hot water and lots of people telling ridiculous stories.

We have been skiing Valle Nevado regularly with our X-Team Clinics since 1999. The skiing ranges from wide-open bowls to backcountry heaven, where steeps and chutes abound. Bring your touring gear and a few extra dollars for the helicopter! The heli-skiing is very inexpensive by North American standards and accesses an incredible range of skiing. We did a couple runs of 5,500 feet of vertical! And did we mention the World Cup race teams? Beginning in August each year, there are usually at least a couple of top European teams training here, an opportunity to see the world's best up close.

Hotel room rates include breakfast, dinner and après-ski tea. This all-inclusive package is a really great European tradition, and it means you don't need to carry any cash at the resort. You can charge all your incidentals, like wine with dinner, to your room. Chilean food is great, especially when whipped up by French chefs.

In Photo 2, the pressure is building onto a solid two-ski platform as Eric rides through the power phase of the turn. In Photo 3, he is reaching for a pole plant and beginning to slowly relax the outside foot and leg. You can just see that the outside leg has gotten shorter and the upper body is moving down the hill. In Photo 4, the skis are coming back under the body as they tip flat to the snow surface.

2

3

4

because wide skis float so much better, we no longer need a precise 50/50 weight split—the outside ski can take more pressure without diving. You can see in this photo that both skis are still cutting cleanly through the turn despite the additional pressure on the outside ski.

In photo 3, Rob has ridden through the turn until his skis begin to cross the hill. Now he begins to slowly relax the outside foot and leg. The rate at which you move your feet here is directly related to your turn radius. Because your turn is a long one, and even though you are going quite fast, you do not want to change edges too quickly. The key is to start the release move very early, before the skis get all the way across the hill—but to do it slowly and smoothly. You want to finish your turn even as you are making the move to get into the next one. Make it a subtle, slow and accurate edge change.

In photos 4 and 5, the relaxation/release naturally draws the legs up as the edge change begins. At the same time, it draws the upper body downhill into the new turn. This is a very natural and effortless movement. The balance is consistent through the neutral phase (photo 5).

From here, Rob leads the edge change by tipping the light, inside foot to the little-toe side. Now he is in perfect position to patiently let the turn develop.

In Photo 5, wide skis and simple movements pay off in spades. When you get to this point, making your next turn is a piece of cake and skiing powder becomes effortless, simple and elegant.

GRAND TARGHEE, WYOMING

Grand Targhee is a true powder gem. The five lifts on two mountains provide access to 2,000 acres of terrain, and you can ride a snowcat to get at another 1,000 acres. It's all angled at the perfect pitch and boasts 500 inches a year of the best powder found anywhere. This makes for huge numbers of awesome powder days every year.

We have been calling Grand Targhee home since we did our first X-Team Clinic there in December 1991. Named for an Indian warrior, it's a self-contained little resort with a country-western charm all its own. It has two hotels, 32 condominium units, and several restaurants ranging from a pizza place to a formal four-star dining room. Back in 1990, the previous owners of the mountain resort heard we were coming to town—and they rebuilt the entire base area!

Targhee is home to the infamous Trap Bar, one of the most happening little après-ski bars we've ever stumbled across (or out of). The place has live music and dancing every afternoon. Each of us has tapped a few tunes on the dance floor with ski boots on.

We've skied Targhee every year since 1991, and we plan to keep going there forever. Eric's son, Wildon, began skiing at Targhee at 18 months.

Grand Targhee's picturesque charm and friendly personality transcend the awesome skiing and great people. You just have to go there and experience it for yourself.

Wide-open spaces and ample powder days after a storm are hallmarks of Targhee.

In crud, good balance and a relaxed, effortless style come from sticking to the essentials of all-mountain skiing. Here's Rob carving in variable, cruddy snow on a north facing notch of Broken Arrow at Squaw Valley.

chapter 3

CRUD SNOW

The most challenging snow of all. crud demands versatility. adaptability and consistency.

The term crud covers a huge variety of snow conditions. Usually it means cut-up, unconsolidated (more loose then packed) snow, often comprised of multiple layers with different densities and textures. Crud is not bad snow. It can be interesting snow, challenging snow. Wide, modern skis turn crud snow into fun snow.

Crud can be warm, heavy snow (which is fun). It can be cold, light snow (which is really fun). It can be wind affected, packed or blown around and deposited (you just never know until you go). It can be breakable crust (no fun at all and potentially dangerous). It can be frozen chicken heads (downright miserable for even the best skiers). It can be dust on crust (fun if the crust is smooth and unbreakable, nasty if it's rough or breakable).

When you get right down to it, crud snow can be anything in the "variable" snow category. The only constant in crud snow skiing is that it will be inconsistent. You can count on having your skis hit different layers of snow or obstacles buried in the snowpack in the course of each run, maybe even in one turn. Each time your skis encounter a change in snow texture, you feel them bounce, decelerate or accelerate. Skiing crud well means staying balanced and consistent while knifing through unpredictable, inconsistent snow.

The goal: balance and consistency

Although crud can be tough and variable, your goal as a skier is the same as anywhere else on the mountain—smoothness. You want to link turns without expending a lot of effort—and you want the ability to change or alter your rhythm and your line at any time. You do this by making two-footed carves with matching edge angles to create a solid two-ski platform. No up-unweighting between turns. Instead, keep your moves simple and consistent, focusing on the essentials, so that your technique itself creates good balance and consistency throughout your turns in this off-piste environment.

Focus first on simplicity. Use the same simple, two-footed movements we have been practicing—with one small, critical adjustment: lower you stance slightly to enhance your ability to absorb inconsistencies in the snowpack at any point in your linked turns. You need to absorb bumps and snowpack inconsistencies to avoid getting thrown or bucked out of your line. To accomplish this objective, your legs and feet have to be able to pump up and down while you focus on tipping your feet and riding your skis.

Your legs need to be relaxed and strong as they pump up and down to manage bumps and keep the skis on the snow while the feet maintain the edge angles to shape your line. In other words, you manage the pressure on the skis with your legs flexing and extending (up and down), while your feet control the lateral (edging and tipping) movements that shape your turns and establish your two-footed carves.

Here you can really see how a good stance allows for up and down movement of the legs to smooth out the ride. In Photo I, Eric is just coming out of a turn. He releases the turn by relaxing his outside foot and leg, which allows both legs to flex up into his stomach to maintain a low center of gravity for better stability. He initiates the edge change by tipping the new inside foot to the little-toe side (Photo 2).

CRUD TOOLS

In crud, you need all the help you can get. In years past, on narrow skis that sank into the junk, even the best skiers needed to break for Mahogany Ridge with the early crew. Today, on wider skis, you can blast through crud all day, buzzer to buzzer.

The wide, shapely profile of modern skis provide a smooth ride. Wide skis float you into the upper layers of the snowpack, minimizing the texture changes you'll encounter. As we explained in previous chapters, this extra float, combined with a turny sidecut, means you need a simple movement pattern to craft great turns. You'll ski better in all conditions with less effort and more control. (Heard this before?)

Another issue to consider in choosing skis for crud: Skis with metal layers generally have more stability and glide speed. You want stability to keep the skis knifing as smoothly as possible through broken snow. You want glide speed to minimize deceleration as you arc from drier snow into wetter stuff. Stability and glide speed are both enhanced by choosing skis with metal (including "Titanal" or steel).

And, especially in wet spring snow, keep 'em waxed.

Coping with adverse or inconsistent snow comes not from varying your technique but from staying true to the movements we have been working on. Two-footed carving, good upper body positioning and calm focus will combine to have you skiing the whole mountain. Here Adam looks marvelous on Spillway at Bolton Valley, Vermont.

The crud stance

Your stance should be similar to your groomed-skiing stance, but even a touch lower to really facilitate the piston-like motion of the legs. How low you want to go can depend on personal preference, but it can also depend on snow conditions. As a rule of thumb, the heavier the snow, the lower you want to be. A low stance puts you in the strongest body position to power the skis through variable snow, which offers more resistance than groomed snow.

At the same time, you do not want to sit so low on your skis that you lean against the back of the boot. This is classic leaning back and would sacrifice balance and control—and also take away from your ability to use the whole ski.

When releasing your turn, it is best to actually retract your legs to create a flat ski float in transition. Try not to extend your legs and launch out of the turn. If your legs go totally straight as you pass through pure neutral in transition, you are vulnerable to being knocked off balance by terrain or snow variations, plus you lose the ability to effectively edge your skis to create the new turn. Instead, stay compact and strong at all times, about halfway between totally extended and completely flexed.

Timing and turn shape

To ski well in cruddy snow, you want to create a two-ski platform with shared weight between your feet. Shift weight to your inside ski by relaxing your outside leg while resisting the build up

This is it: Perfect body position. The real key is the position of his hips relative to his feet. Notice that his hips are slightly behind his feet to enhance the up and down movement of his legs (as shock absorbers) while maintaining the shin to boot contact needed to stay forward.

Hard snow underneath soft snow tests the durability of Rob's skis as he powers through a high-speed carve. Even under this intense pressure, Rob is in perfect position to handle it. His legs are positioned for power and flexibility, and his upper body is centered towards his next turn.

Here's Rob finishing a short turn in Photo I and releasing the turn in Photo 2. His legs move up as he comes over a little rollover, with his new inside foot tipping into the new turn. In Photo 4, his legs extend a bit to maintain snow contact, but there is no twisting of the feet.

of forces with the inside foot and leg as needed to create the two-ski platform through each turn.

The move of relaxing the outside foot and leg also triggers the release of the turn. As you flow into the new turn, focus on the same basic footwork we have been working on. Do not twist the skis to turn them and stay patient and poised in transition. Continue the tipping movement of the new inside foot to lead the edge change and shape the top of the new turn. If possible, maintain snow contact at all times. This is not critical to success but will definitely smooth out the ride and maximize efficiency entering the new turn.

In addition to balance, speed control is key to a good time in this type of snow. Speed control comes mainly from turn shape. The more

you get the skis across the fall line (hill) at the end of each turn, the more you will slow down. You can finish your turns either hard or soft.

A hard finish provides a strong turning force, so the skis carve the entire arc. This type of turn is like a railroad track—the shovel of each ski sets the groove (in the snow) for the rest of ski to follow through the arc.

In a soft finish, you complete the turn by "shaving" the skis across the snow surface. This graceful, versatile move provides a relaxed release and flow through transition and into the new turn with balance and control. Trigger the soft finish by downweighting softly (flexing your legs) or sinking lower as you pass through the fall line, thus breaking your tails loose. We'll discuss this in more detail below.

Medium-radius turn in crud

This is a really good turn for the new, wider skis. It will become your "money" turn for crud snow. It works well in any snow condition and at a variety of speeds. Fast or slow, it can give you balanced, linked turns, all with the same core movement pattern.

Photo 1: Ride both skis through the finish of the turn, absorbing bumps as needed. To release your turn and flow into the next, relax your outside leg even if you're weighting your feet more equally.

Photo 2 and 3: As you transfer to the new edges (by tipping the new, lightly weighted inside foot to the little-toe side), maintain snow contact if you can, especially with the uphill foot. Do not twist or oversteer your skis. Just focus on guiding your new inside ski lightly onto edge in the new turn while maintaining a low stance.

Photo 4: Have patience, patience, and more patience as your skis seek the fall line. Your only real activity here is to tip your feet progressively onto edge to cut the snow and carve into the new turn. Keep your stance relatively low for better stability and balance. Also, do not overpressure the skis with forward pressure (no aggressively pressing your ankles against the tongues of your boots) or premature downweighting or sinking onto the skis. Let this top part of the turn happen largely on its own, with the upper body directed right into the middle of the new turn. Stay balanced in the middle of the

Eric has just released the old turn (Photo 4) and started the new turn by lifting the downhill foot and tipping it to the new turn angle. Notice how the upper body has already moved into the new turn. In Photos 5-6, the key is to have patience and let the skis come around naturally.

ski, focusing on the light inside foot tipped onto the little-toe edge. And do not lean back.

Photo 5: The turn comes around, you are arcing into the fall line, and your weight is settling onto the skis. As in powder, you are poised to create a one- or two-ski platform, depending on the snow texture. The firmer the snow, the more you can choose between one ski or two to support your weight and set the edges in the arc. In deeper snow, you need a two-ski platform to prevent the dominant ski from diving.

Photo 6: Either way, as you arc through the turn, control your speed through turn shape. To slow down, you need to get your skis all the way across the fall line. This is the point in your turn where the G forces are really building up. Settle your G's right onto the skis in a "hard" carve and power through the finish, relying solely on your turn for speed control. The other option is to finish the turn more softly (detailed below).

The soft finish
The other option you have is the soft finish of the turn, which works well on corn snow, firm surfaces and in deeper snow where the upper layers are fairly light. The trick is to shape your carve by downweighting softly to break your ski tails loose into a controlled, shaped slide. The soft finish is very smooth. It doesn't create the huge buildup of G forces you get in a pure carved turn. It's therefore easier to manage, especially for skiers who tire quickly. We also

If you've used the basic all-mountain skills and been patient up to this point (Photos 4-6, previous page), you will finish the turn in balance and in control.

use this feathered turn often when skiing very fast, to brake a bit before negotiating a tight notch or other terrain problem.

The transition phase of the turn is identical to the hard-finish turn. It's just that your skis aren't cutting a true carving arc. Instead, they "shave" a smooth, crescent-moon shaped track. The ski shovel sets the direction, but the tails don't follow right in that same track. When the tails break loose, they push the surface snow sideways, absorbing energy and scrubbing off some speed. You can do this effectively, because you entered the turn in balance, with the skis at matching edge angles.

When you finish the turn softly like this, you make the same release move we have been talking about. Release this turn by relaxing the outside leg and retracting both feet to transfer to the new turn. This will trigger the same smooth and effortless release into the new turn. The key to knowing you did this right is when you feel the same effortless link between turns. You should be able to look back up the hill and see a nice crescent-moon-shaped track, and then two clean ski tracks coming out the bottom and disappearing into the transition. The two ski tracks will start again right away in the next turn.

TRICKS OF THE CRUDMEISTERS

Recoveries: Use your inside ski as a recovery aid whenever your outside ski bounces out of its expected arc. This actually happens a lot in crud snow—it's standard operating procedure. To recover, just push down on your inside ski (as you pull in the outside one), hold yourself up, and keep the turn going. Once your outside ski comes back into position to finish the turn, then you can shift your weight very easily back onto that dominant ski—just take the weight off the inside ski. Finish the turn riding a two-ski platform again, and then to release into the next turn.

Airplane turn: As you dial in your crud turns, it's a lot of fun to mix it up and play with your turns a bit. A really fun transition move is to use a bump (either in the snowpack or maybe a terrain roll) to trigger your transition, and then lay it out into an airplane turn. Just as you hit the bump, retract your legs and catch a little lift off the bump. As you are floating through the air, change edges by tipping the inside foot to the little-toe side. You also want to steer your skis slightly towards the fall line so that when you touch down with both skis on edge, you are landing in the turn and your skis immediately begin to arc together in a solid two-ski platform.

Long turns: Make more long-radius turns than short ones. On your wide skis, once you get the hang of the longer turn, you will be way more efficient. You will flow down the mountain a little differently.

Seek the good stuff: Finally, explore the mountain and try to find the best snow. Crud is often the stuff you're left with a couple of days after a storm. All the fresh snow is skied out, or sun and wind have put the snow into a transition phase. Still, you'll find better snow in some places than others. Consider elevation, aspect to the sun, aspect to the wind, slope angle and open areas or trees, then try to find the best snow you can. Drier, colder snow (up higher on the mountain, or sheltered from the sun on a northern exposure) is often lighter. Snow in lee gullies (protected from the wind) is often deeper. Experiment with different areas of the mountain on your own, or better yet, follow an experienced local. Just make sure you can keep up with her!

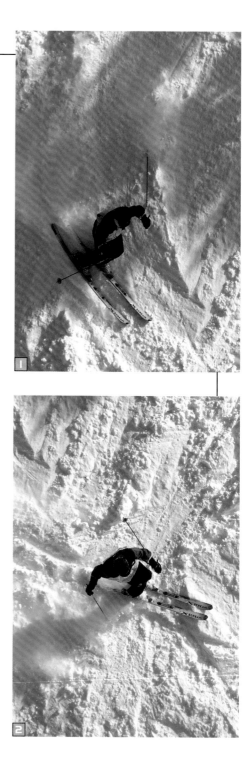

Short-radius turns in crud

There was a time when everyone made short turns in crud and chopped-up snow. Some skiers still make it their turn of choice. The short turn works in all snow conditions, and there are times when it's the only way to go—such as in firm or frozen crud and breakable crust, where long-radius, high-speed turns are nothing but trouble. Short-radius turns with effective speed control can handle just about anything, so the turn needs to be in your quiver of moves. However, for most unconsolidated snow conditions, skiing with short-radius hip-hop turns is really tiring.

Stance: Faced with a long section of short-radius turns, you need to manage your energy so you don't end up exhausted. This means you should plan to take advantage of the snow's texture to help flex your skis into each arc. In heavier crud snow, your stance should be slightly on your heels through the loaded, bottom portion of the turn, and then slightly forward in transition. This forward stance is very subtle and can be accomplished simply by pulling the feet back under the hips just a touch as the feet pass through the neutral zone. In light crud snow, like chopped-up powder, your stance should be pretty well centered. As your speed increases, your stance may want to drift just a touch back so you are less likely to overturn the skis. The upper body should face right into the middle of the next turn (in this case of short radius turns, straight down the hill).

Timing: Use the same fundamental movement pattern to create nice, quick turns. A short-

See how the skis have come around to line back up with the upper body—and how both skis are tracking together.

ROLE OF THE UPPER BODY

Good upper body positioning through the end of every turn is one of the fundamental elements of sound skiing. Good upper body position sets you up perfectly to flow into your next turn with balance and poise.

Your eyes and shoulders need to face the middle of your next turn—that is, the direction you're moving down the hill. This is not always where your skis are pointing, especially in the late part of the turn.

This deviation—skis running across the slope, upper body oriented more downhill—creates a twisting or coiling effect in your hips and midsection. You are "loading the spring." To understand this better, try this: sit in a swivel chair at your desk or at a table. Sit normally, with your back straight but with your feet just off the floor. Now twist your legs around to the side while you hold on to your desk with both hands. Pretend your computer screen is your line of descent. Hold this position with your shoulders pointing forward—it takes effort.

Now, relax those muscles that hold you. What happens? Your feet and legs swing back into alignment with your eyes, shoulders and upper body.

The same thing happens when you are skiing on modern skis.

When your shoulders are facing into your next turn and the spring is coiled, the moment you release your edges your skis will naturally seek the fall line, beginning your transition phase. This really sets you up in perfect position to power through every turn.

With proper upper body positioning, your pole plant is mainly for timing. Plant your pole and relax your downhill foot and leg to release your turn.

Quiet amid the chaos. Rob's upper body is solid and his eyes calmly focused downhill as his legs and skis do all the work in this long-radius ripper.

radius crud turn starts at the end of the previous turn, with a quick edge set to make a crisp finish to the turn. A quick downweighting and slight push on the skis to get a sharp edge set, then release the turn right away with a quick leg retraction movement. The release should be in tempo with the quickness of the edge set. This movement needs to be dynamic—relax or take weight off the outside foot, and then quickly retract both feet and draw the new inside foot towards the new outside foot, thereby leading the edge change movement.

Long-radius turns in crud

The long-radius crud turn is a relatively new phenomenon for average skiers, only becoming feasible with the invention of wide skis. High-speed crud turns on narrow skis were often an invitation to disaster. Today, on wider skis, and for really good skiers, there seems to be a speed threshold—once you pass it, the ride on the modern skis grows smoother. In effect, wide skis let you hydroplane on the snowpack, skimming through the top layers. This works in a wide range of unconsolidated snow types. Firm crud is a different story. High-speed turns on a rough crust may produce nothing but a rattley ride into oblivion. Sometimes you just have to do the best you can to absorb the hard bumps and try to maintain your arc. If you can keep your edges on the snow, you may be able to control your speed.

So let's focus on high speeds in unconsolidated snow. First, understand that deep crud is much more difficult on narrow skis (by which we mean skis with a waist width of 70mm or less). Even a narrow shaped ski (with a wide shovel and tail and narrow waist) is unpredictable and jumpy at speed in crud, and harder to manage at slower speeds as well. A narrow waist sinks deeper under foot, so you will get bucked around by the variable layers. This makes it tough to maintain fore-aft balance. Basically, if you're not right on the sweet spot of the skis and well balanced, you will get tossed all over the place. Your margin for error is relatively small—and the consequences of being just a bit out of balance are much greater then if you were on a wider profile ski. With modern, wider skis, you can ride over or through just about any conditions, and have fun doing it.

Anatomy of a high-speed crud ripper. Photos 1-2: Rob comes into the power phase of the turn aligned and poised to handle the big G's. Photos 3-4: He releases the turn by bringing his new inside foot towards his outside foot to set up the new turn.

Dynamic stance: As in powder snow, the main difference from groomed technique is that the high-speed stance is critical. Keep your shins against the tongues of your boots, your legs flexed pretty low and your shoulders centered above your feet and knees. You need to be able to absorb shocks, stay in balance, maintain edge angles and make smooth lateral movement, all at the same time.

Think of your body as the suspension system of a car—it allows the wheels to turn and at the same time handle bumps. For a car, handling the bumps is really a two-part action. First there is up movement of the wheel, to absorb the impact of the bump. Then there is down movement, the springs pushing the wheel back down on the road to maintain grip in the corners. It is the same thing here in skiing.

Photo 1: Rob is coming throught the fall line balanced and poised, ready for the G's of this big turn.

Photo 2: Rob is the bottom of the turn, standing balanced and powering the skis through the arc. The legs are absorbing and pushing back in flowing movement to hold the skis on the snow and in the arc. The legs can work together, or more independently, as needed at any moment.

Photo 3: Rob starts to release the turn by relaxing the outside leg. As usual, this triggers the transition and transfers weight on to the uphill ski, loading it to flow onto the new turning edge and start the next turn.

Photo 4: The inside ski leads the edge change as always, coming in light and tipping into the new turn. The big trick here is to stay poised and patient. Stay centered in your high-speed stance to handle the variable snow and keep both skis tracking together.

Control your speed through turn shape. Even in long-radius turns, you can finish any turn with a hard carve or a soft carve, depending on the snow and terrain.

In a spot like this, it's all about turn placement. The turn before this is the key to hitting the mark. Here's Eric in the Palisades at Sugar Bowl, California.

Calm focus and flawless execution got Rob safely down this frozen, 50-plus-degree couloir at le Brevent above Chamonix, France.

chapter 4

STEEPS

Skiing steeps is as much about mental attitude as technique. It's about weighing your ability—and your desire—against the reality of the snow and the mountain.

What is it about steep skiing that makes it so exciting and scary—and so much friggin' fun to do?

To us it's the satisfaction of facing a challenge. In each run on truly steep terrain, there's a zen-like moment when your focus is so acute that it's almost a form of meditation. To succeed you must execute precise movements with refined balance. Skiing well on steep slopes is the ultimate achievement for any expert skier.

Skiing steeps is also liberating. When you can comfortably and safely execute steep turns, the terrain barriers fall. You can really ski the whole mountain—one of the hallmarks of the expert skier. You will be able to ski the best areas of any mountain—the routes that separate the expert from the intermediate.

Evaluating the risks

Risk plays a considerable part in the challenge of skiing steep slopes. This is not to say that all steep slopes are dangerous. But when the slope reaches a certain angle of steepness, something in the mind shifts, and the hill is no longer benign. You really have to pay attention and execute your movements accurately. The margin for error is slim.

Most skiers would agree that a slope is steep when it affects your technique. Steepness becomes a challenge when it makes you defensive. You need to push through the anxiety—the steep skier needs accuracy in technique without thought or emotion. You need a clear focus, an awareness of the environment (especially of the snow and slope), and an eagerness to thrive on the challenge. As the risk increases, the satisfaction grows.

The slope angle and the snow conditions affect the hazard level. On hard snow, you will pick up speed very quickly in the transition between turns. The consequences of any fall can be severe: a high-speed slide on firm or frozen snow can result in serious injury or death. The real threat is not the slide itself, but the likelihood of colliding with a fixed object—a tree, a series of big moguls, a lift tower, a rock, or a crevasse. You could sail off a cliff. Not good either.

On large mountains with heavy snowfall, avalanches become a real risk on slopes between 28 and 50 degrees (we will come back to this issue). Generally, anything below 28 degrees is not steep enough to slide, and slopes over 50 degrees usually self-control during storms—that is, loose snow slides off almost as it accumulates. Any pitch over 50 degrees should be skied only by very experienced steep skiers, with the skill and savvy to handle it. Unfortunately, that dangerous 28-to-50-degree zone is the perfect range of steepness that we all love to ski.

Who doesn't take the occasional Dixie? The trick is to pick your upsets carefully: Never upend where a slide might kill you.

Be realistic. The fact is that you have fallen, and that you will fall again. So in evaluating the hazards of any slope, the real question is,

Sometimes pulling off a crux move depends on the set-up turns coming into it. Here's Rob setting up to minimize the hazard by airing the whole mess.

Rob looking small among giant boulders. The California spring skiing season is the longest and best in the world.

"What if I fall here?" Identify what presents the risk to your overall health and decide if you are up to the challenge at that moment.

Where it's really steep, we humans venture out of our natural element. This is where we must humble ourselves before the greatness of the mountains. The mountain is what it is, and we are at the mercy of the existing conditions. There is no question of mastering the mountain. The great French extreme skier Sylvain Saudan once said, "All I can do is to master myself."

As the slopes get steeper and longer, the danger increases. Recognizing and evaluating the hazards presented by the mountain is a key component to a long and prosperous steep-skiing existence.

In evaluating the hazards in any run, there are three main elements to consider:
- Slope angle (How steep is it?)
- Snow conditions (Is it hard or soft? Is it stable?)
- Terrain configuration (If I fall, will I slide into rocks? Over cliffs? Or out onto a gentle concave bowl?)

It is up to you to evaluate these factors, define the challenge being presented by the mountain on this particular run and then make a decision you can live with. Literally. If you are on a steep, moguly pitch that runs a short distance on frozen snow, you are on a pitch with a hazard lower then a longer pitch with no bumps that runs for 1000 feet above a crevassed glacier. It is not rocket science but you need to make this type of reasoning a part of your decision making process when evaluating a particular run and making a decision to ski or not to ski. Remember, you can always come back and ski it another day.

Also, trust your gut instincts. If you get to the top of a steep run and, for no good reason you just do not feel right about skiing, then don't ski it! Trust your instincts.

Photo 1: **Lift your heel towards your butt just as the ski comes off the snow so you don't catch the tail on the steep slope.** Photo 2: **A good solid carve feels great on good snow. Notice how Eric's upper body is curled out over the downhill ski to increase the bite.**

Steep technique

The steep technique is not much different from the movements you use on moderate terrain. You'll still rely on the essential movements of sound all-mountain skiing. The main modification: Steep skiing requires more of a "pedal" move in transition—that is, an active switch in leg length during the transition, mimicking the action of pedaling a bicycle.

The goal is to minimize the vertical drop between edge-sets, and therefore minimize the time you accelerate in free-fall as you get from the control phase of one turn to the control phase of the next. The bottom of the turn is the control phase, where you need to achieve a very efficient setting of the edge to control speed and maintain the option to stop completely if necessary.

To release the turn and flow into the next, there is an active weight shift onto the uphill ski, created by retracting the downhill foot as you actively extend the uphill leg. As the downhill foot is retracting and you are pushing off with the uphill leg, you want to immediately tip your new inside foot decisively toward its little-toe edge (down the hill), so you lead the edge change with this light foot. This movement will draw you down the slope, naturally releasing the uphill foot and ski to flow through transition and become the weighted outside ski in the new turn.

You can finish the turn in three different ways to control your speed:

• a hard edge set

Good spring snow can be the best, most predictable snow for really steep skiing. Here Eric sets up for a new turn up above a small bergschrund where the snow is starting to creep downhill away from the ridge line.

- a hard or definitive carve or
- a softer finish, like the one we looked at in the crud chapter and in the photos at right.

In all cases, maintaining speed control is the key. It's safe practice to complete each turn with a subtle down-weighting move to shave the snow and shape a round, speed-control finish. With good technique and stable balance, this control phase of the turn sets up your next turn. In fact, as you are finishing one turn you can decide what type of turn you will use next, based on the pitch and snow surface. We'll discuss the three types of turns a little later in more detail.

Upper body position

The upper body has a specialized role to play in steeps: It has to stay over the feet at all times throughout your series of linked turns. It has to stay centered over the feet in each transition and through each turn finish. This is necessary to create focused, consistent and natural loading of the skis for edge grip, and for seamless links between turns.

Good upper body centering is the biggest single sticking point for people who have problems in steep terrain. If this is a problem for you, focus on getting the shoulders centered over the downhill foot and ski through the control phase of each turn. To do it, you'll have to lean out over the downhill foot at the end of every turn. This is a big issue, because the natural reaction of the brain and body on a steep slope is to lean uphill (into the slope) away from that dreadful pitch. And that uphill lean

This is a really nice set-up turn, with hands, eyes and shoulders pointing right down the line to arc through the rocks. Location: Treble Cone, New Zealand.

The trademark of Squaw Valley is a lift system that provides uphill transportation to every nook and cranny the mountain has to offer.

SQUAW VALLEY

Squaw Valley is one of those magical places that has everything a skier could want. If you grew up in the East like we did—and you love to ski—then Squaw Valley is a dream come true. Not only are the Sierra Nevada mountains bigger than anything in Vermont, but the resort itself could fit every ski area in Chittenden County inside it. Not only is there twice as much snow annually, but it's sunny four out of five days. Not only is there no ice, but THERE IS NO ICE. So it wasn't a difficult decision to stay when we got there in the fall of '88—after stopping in Colorado, Utah and New Mexico on the way.

But there was more to it than that. During the mid eighties, "extreme skiing" was getting pretty popular. Scot Schmidt and Tom Day were performing for Warren Miller in a zone at Squaw called "the Palisades," which was touted as the new breeding ground for exterminators. After seeing some of the footage and agreeing that "we could do that," the brothers DesLauriers headed for Tahoe.

After years of skiing and traveling all over the world, our opinion is that Squaw is world-class. Every region in the world has its good and bad points, of course, and there are always places that outclass Squaw in one way or another. But when it comes down to it, Squaw as a whole is one nifty package.

First, let's talk about the myth of "Sierra Cement." There are two words for all those nay-sayers in Utah: Fat skis. Problem solved. And there are a plethora of other two-word catch phrases that are related: Stable snowpack, sunny weather, regular beer, and plentiful backcountry, to mention a few.

Secondly, the caliber of skiers and snowboarders at Squaw Valley is like nowhere else. This is no exaggeration. After skiing in Europe, Canada, Alaska, South America, Asia and all over the U.S., it's still awe-inspiring to ride KT-22 on a powder day. Everywhere you look, you'll see death-defying ski stunts performed by people who have never been anywhere near a ski movie shoot.

The vibe is contagious. Even the people that aren't in the movies and the magazines are passionate about skiing, and they put it on display at Squaw Valley. These people pound nails or swab paint brushes seven days a week during the off-season so they can ski every single day of the ski season at Squaw. There are ski bums everywhere, but these people never leave. The corps of old-timers that ski top-to-bottom KT-22 laps all day, every day are testimony to this. These people are in their fifties and sixties and still live to ski Squaw every single day. It's not a ski area, it's a way of life.

Of course, there are plenty of rock stars at Squaw, too. It's been said that if you throw a snowball in Squaw, you'll hit a ski movie star. It's no coincidence. These people are professionals, and they've done their research. The terrain and the weather around Lake Tahoe are definitely some of the world's greatest. And if you want a gaggle of lifts that will take you there, Squaw is second to none.

The KT-22 high-speed quad at Squaw Valley (in the background) provides the best skiing of any one chairlift in North America, accessing three distinct bowls with multiple aspects to ensure good skiing all season.

Here's an old-school hop turn getting the job done on a 52-degree shoulder of the Palisades in Squaw Valley. This picture was taken when we used this turn a lot more than we do now.

is just what you can't afford, because it reduces your edge grip. Of the numerous ways you can lose it in the steeps, this is the most common.

Three variations of the steep turn

There are basically three variations of the steep turn. They differ mainly in the transition phase and the amount of snow contact through the turn itself. These are: 1) the pedal hop (facing page), 2) the pedal hop-carve (this page); and 3) the full-snow-contact pedal carve (next page). On any given slope, the versatile skier might use all three types of turns as the terrain and snow change.

A good example of a run which lends itself to a mix of these three steep turns is the classic hourglass-shaped Alta 1 Chute (skier's left line) at Jackson Hole, Wyoming. It starts out wide open, then funnels through a crux move, and opens back up at the bottom. An experienced, confident skier could start this run with long radius, snow-contact carving turns, progressively shortening the turns to slalom-sized snow-contact short turns. As the funnel necks down to the crux, just 200cm wide, you need to tighten up to pedal hop-carves, then to pedal hops. Then, as the chute opens into Laramie Bowl, you can progressively open it back it up to GS-length turns.

An aspiring steep skier should approach any funneling route conservatively, using pedal carves right from the start to control the speed. That's because a high-speed long-radius carved turn at the top can easily turn into a high speed crash right into the rocks, through the funnel.

As you become more comfortable with the pedal movement, you can advance to this turn on open steep slopes. This "pedal carve" turn uses very little hop or lifting of the skis and can be done with very little effort.

Bottom line: Choose the turn that fits your level of skill as well as the nature of the terrain.

Think of linked turns as an "S" shape. In steeps the "safe zone," the control phase of each turn, is the bottom or horizontal end of each curve in the S. The goal in steeps is to minimize effort and maximize control as you move from safe zone to safe zone. You are slow and safe when the control phase of the turn is exaggerated and the transition is short.

The pure pedal turn is one of the safest old-school ways for good skiers to ski the steeps. It's a simple jump from the bottom of one turn to the bottom of the next, essentially performing the top and middle of each turn in the air. If total control is your only consideration, this is an effective, but exhausting, technique. When the terrain is less than life-threatening, or as you gain confidence on your skis, you can make more and more of that steep turn on the snow: Hop only to the fall line of the next turn and then quickly arc around into the safe zone. Or hop only the edge change itself, and make a full and quick turn on the snow. Now let's discuss the essentials of the three steep techniques.

ENTRY CONTROL

The first turn of a steep run is always the toughest one, and it seems that, statistically speaking, it's also where you are most likely to cross your tips and Dixie down the slope. If you are a good skier who gets nervous in steeps or has a hard time getting a difficult run started, here's some advice to start you off.

There are two ways to ski a steep slope: exceedingly fast or not exceedingly fast. For even good skiers, exceedingly fast can mean eventual trouble. A common mistake is to make a complete turn at the outset, which means your first move is to float the skis into the fall line. Because you haven't already dropped into the coiled stance, that first transition is a looong one, and you can easily pick up a ton of speed. If you're not ready for this sudden acceleration, you start your run struggling for control. This can be really scary on a big slope, especially when your second edge set is made by the side of your butt, not the edges of your skis.

The easy solution is to make your first turn a half-turn, so that your skis do not go straight into the fall line. This is especially useful on variable snow and in tight or unfamiliar terrain. It helps you to get a feel for the snow and helps to set a rhythm for your run right away. You can see in the photos that in this case a quick turn into the fall line would mean either jamming back into the rock or pointing 'em down and straightlining out of frame (which wasn't really an option here).

Photo 1: Instead, the tactic was to let the skis drift slightly downhill to get onto the and then make a crescent moon shaped turn right across the hill in the same general direction the skis started in.

Photo 2: Once you have the edges setting, you can even feather this turn (by slightly releasing the edges) to get a better feel for the slope, lose a little vertical and really set you up to flow into your next turn.

This move sets up your balanced stance so you can flow into your first real turn (which actually is your second edge set) with confidence and poise—and ready to set up a rhythm.

The move is also ideal for getting off a cornice or entering a chute.

A close-up the feet when initiating the hop movement. The tips diverge as you hop off the uphill foot. Remember to hop just enough so you can steer the skis into the fall line and bring the new inside ski in close to the outside one so both skis touch back down together in parallel.

Pedal hop turn, the essentials

The dynamics of the pedal hop turn is similar to skipping along a sidewalk. When you skip, you jump off—and land—on the same foot. Same thing with the pedal hop or "skip" turn: Jump off and land on the dominant (outside) foot in the turn. This is the key to skiing the steeps.

The pedal hop turn is the most difficult of the three turns, because it requires the most energy, but it is critically important. You may end up using this turn only in very specific situations—but there will be times when you'll need it.

The key is efficiency in the hopping and skipping movement. Focus on lifting the feet and retracting them towards your body to conserve energy. More specifically: Focus on lifting your heel toward your butt. Avoid moving your upper body upward too much.

Photo 1: Start the move by transferring all your weight to the little-toe edge of your uphill ski—simply by taking your weight off your downhill foot. Retract your downhill leg to lift this foot off the snow. Your uphill leg is now your new dominant turning leg.

Photo 2: This new dominant leg is flexed and packed with potential energy. Tap that potential by pushing off and hopping just enough to lift your heels and skis off the snow. This heel lift is key, because it brings your skis parallel to the slope as you pivot them into the new turn.

Photo 3: When your skis are parallel to the snow, you only need a few inches of elevation to pivot your ankles and complete the turn. The heel lift also helps you maintain dynamic balance through the turn by moving your upper body down the hill appropriately with the turn. Also, as you are pedaling, you should lead your edge change by tipping the lifted inside foot to its new turning edge as you float patiently through the transition.

Lastly, land with your skis on edge and

Minimize your hop to be most efficient. Stay relatively compact like Eric is. Notice how he does not extend too much and hops just enough to get his skis onto their new turning edges.

pointing almost all the way across the fall line into the safe zone of the new turn. On landing, most if not all of your weight is on the dominant outside foot, especially on firm snow.

With the turn complete, transfer the weight to the uphill ski (the new dominant foot) and repeat. Develop a rhythm. As you practice this turn, pretend you're in a tight, steep chute, where you need bombproof speed control. Keep practicing it until you can do it with little or no chattering skid.

Pedal hop-carve turn, the essentials

With the same mechanics as in the pedal turn above, hop off that uphill (new dominant turning) ski into the fall line and complete the carve quickly on the snow. This time, focus more on the essential element of foot tipping (getting the skis onto their new turning edges) quicker in the transition. This will create carving action immediately upon touchdown.

Photo 1 (this page): Transfer weight to the uphill, dominant turning ski by lightening and lifting the downhill ski to release the turn.

Photo 2: Then tip that newly unweighted ski down the hill as you begin your "skip" to the fall line. Remember to jump off and land on that same foot and to project your body out from and down the slope towards your new turn. Now, the idea is to tip your feet into the new turn as you lift your skis parallel to the snow surface and pivot them into the fall line.

Photo 3: Focus on leading this edge change move with the new inside foot. By lifting and tipping this way, you are dynamically balanced and on edged skis as you land. Right where you want to be.

Photo 4: Keep your inside ski light on the snow as you touch down. From this balanced position you can complete the turn into that "safe zone" instantaneously.

Focus on staying forward with your eyes looking at the middle of your next turn. It is exactly the same as making a short-radius turn on the groomed runs. Avoid leaning back and twisting your skis into the new turn. Focus on the essentials.

Pedal carve turn, the essentials

Now, the easiest variation of all. This time, you only hop the edge change itself (from little-toe edge to big-toe edge) on the uphill (new dominant turning foot). Then you complete the arc on the snow. Key principles still apply: Keep your upper body facing the middle of your new turn.

Photo 1: To release your turn, take your weight off the downhill foot to transfer weight to the uphill foot/edge, and begin the pedal unweighting.

Photo 2: Hop only the edge change itself, by now lifting your uphill heel off the snow. Lead the edge change by tipping the new inside foot to its little-toe edge as it continues the pedal move.

Photo 3: In this little hop, slightly lightening the heel creates tip pressure which, combined with the side cut of shaped skis and the tipping of the edges, drives the ski into a tight carve.

Photo 4: Finish this turn by carving through your arc with the inside ski light and aggressively tipped into the hill.

Sound familiar? Good.

STEEP AND DEEP

In one respect, skiing steep powder is a lot like skiing moderate-slope powder: To do it well, you have to have patience while skiing a slightly longer turn than you would on a firm surface. When you release the turn to flow into the new one, you have to allow your skis to come up and out of the snow. This longer release allows your skis to get out of the snow as you pedal-turn and tip the skis onto their new turning edges. Don't try to pedal and twist your skis at the same time, or you'll quickly work yourself into a sweating mess. Have patience in the transition and accomplish your speed control at the bottom of each arc, in the natural control phase of the turn. Realize that despite the steep pitch, the deep snow itself will slow you down through the natural resistance it offers your skis. The heavier the snow, the more resistance it will have.

Notice how much vertical Eric takes up between these photos. When there is plenty of hill to work with, make a slightly longer turn than you think you should.

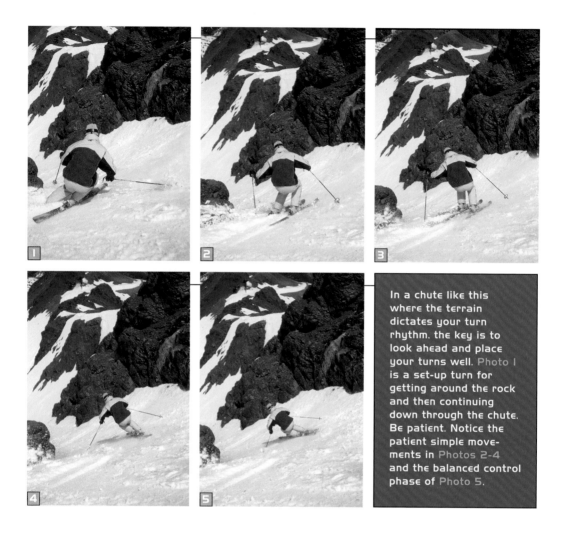

In a chute like this where the terrain dictates your turn rhythm, the key is to look ahead and place your turns well. Photo 1 is a set-up turn for getting around the rock and then continuing down through the chute. Be patient. Notice the patient simple movements in Photos 2-4 and the balanced control phase of Photo 5.

Which turn to use

OK, now a little secret: Those weren't drills at all, but real variations on true steep turns. You can hop or carve any amount of any steep turn. What you decide to do depends on the terrain, the snow and situation. Here are the basic guidelines:

Tight turns in narrow chutes on relatively firm snow: Hop most or all of the turn. In other words, complete most of your turn in the air.

Semi-open steeps with dry snow or spring corn: Hop the top half of the turn only and complete the turn with carving action.

Open steeps with dry snow, corn snow, or a powder coating over a carveable surface: Pedal/hop the edge change only and work the skis through a full carve.

Anatomy of a couloir

The French word couloir literally means corridor or passage. In the mountains, a couloir is a narrow channel between rock walls. You find couloirs in various shapes and sizes all over the world,

MOMENT OF TRUTH

The mental problem in skiing steeps often appears right after the pole plant, during the instant when your skis flow underneath you and onto their new turning edges. This requires a brief moment of confidence and patience—confidence that your skis will, in fact, flow onto edge and make the turn, and the patience to allow it to happen. If you pass through this moment with good balance, you will make a beautiful carved turn and have good control. But if you rush it by over-steering your skis into the turn, or if you delay it by shying away from the fall line, then you will skid and lose control. This is true in all skiing, but the problem is amplified on steeps.

Photo 1: Eric is at the end of one turn, in a stable and balanced position. In the next moment, his body stays centered over his skis and moves down the hill. This is the critical interval.

Photo 2: Eric patiently maintains his balanced position throughout; his skis have flowed from one set of edges to the other as he moves confidently down the hill.

Photo 3: Because he's patient and committed to the fall line early in the turn, he is able to carve and complete the turn as the G's build.

Footwork speed should relate to your turn radius, not to your actual downhill velocity. In short tight turns your feet move quickly under your body, onto the new edges and into the next turn. In longer turns, even though your speed is faster, your feet move a little slower—so you need even more patience.

If you can ski well on groomed slopes, you can handle the terrain in this sequence. You just have to pass through this moment of truth (not necessarily in the air) depicted in Photos 2 and 3 (no problem). From here it is easy to finish your turn in balance and achieve the control you are seeking.

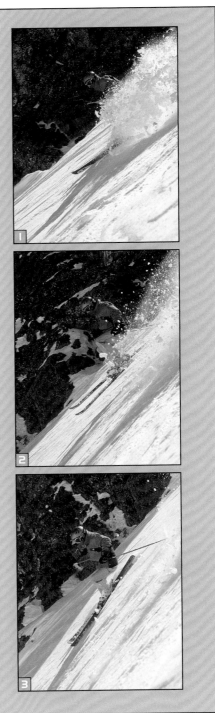

Skiing a big couloir in Chamonix (or anywhere else) is a multi-stage experience. This is the Couloir des Poubelles off the Grand Montet in Chamonix. The couloir runs for a good 2,000 vertical feet from the top of the Belvedere gondola. Before embarking on a run like this, make sure you have the right gear, the right friends and the right knowledge of the route to know what to expect.

Photo 1: Getting into the couloir is fun. Most people rappel down using a rope affixed to a steel post at the top.

Photo 2: This photo was taken at the very top looking down at the skinny part of the run in the dog-leg. Here Eric makes a controlled pedal turn in the soft snow. It's quite a thrill just looking down a line like this.

Photo 3 shows Eric making a full-on hop turn to negotiate the tight dog-leg section. The average pitch of this run is about 42-45 degrees. Not too steep, but steep enough that you want to stay in control.

Photo 4: The middle of the couloir. Deano is stretching his legs in a nice little hop turn. Check out the beautiful section of the run below as it opens up on the moraine above the Valle Blanche.

At right: The reward for a job well done.

from the Selkirks to the Sierra, from the Alps to the Himalaya. Some are straight fall line shots. Some have one or more bends—vertical dog-legs. In the U.S., a short couloir is usually termed a chute. The famous Alta Chutes at Jackson Hole are steep and narrow, lined by rocks or trees, but they're only about 300 feet long. In comparison, Corbet's Couloir, on the some mountain, is called a couloir because it's lined by major rock walls and is over 1,000 feet long. But even Corbet's is dwarfed by couloirs in the Alps, where some have more than a mile of vertical drop. These are amazing places to be on skis, places that make you feel both humble and happy.

For us, skiing in a couloir transcends all other types of skiing. With cliffs soaring above you on both sides, it feels as if the mountain is wrapping its arms around you. It's very quiet in a couloir: The only sounds are those you make yourself. Once you begin to relax in this environment, you feel a peacefulness you don't get anywhere else in the mountains. But there is still that element of risk that makes you feel vibrantly alive.

Descending a couloir is like skiing in a funnel. Once you're in, you're committed. It's usually not feasible to climb back out unless you have mountaineering equipment in your pack. Round turns are mandatory if you don't want to run into the rock walls. If an avalanche should occur, there's little or no room to get out of its path. That's why, even in a not-too-steep couloir, deciding whether it's safe is the first priority. Licensed guides in places like Chamonix have the knowledge and experience to make this evaluation for you. When you're on your own, couloir survival depends on your understanding

CHAMONIX

Cradled between some of the most spectacular mountains in the world lies the magical town of Chamonix, France. We've skied all over the world, but have yet to find a ski resort as enchanting and thrilling as Chamonix.

Chamonix would captivate anyone. The surrounding mountains, rising to over 15,000 feet offer endless adventure: world renowned skiing, climbing, and paragliding, to name a few. Whether you're an intrepid mountaineer seeking a challenge, or a novice skier searching for mellow yet exciting slopes, Chamonix satisfies all appetites. Nothing is more romantic than enjoying the spectacular scenery from an outdoor cafe, sipping a soul-warming cup of vin chaud (hot wine). After a beautiful day of skiing, we love to relax with friends, drinking grolle (hot spiced wine served in an earthenware pot) and swapping stories.

Chamonix is widely known as the birthplace of mountaineering .

You could spend a lifetime exploring what Chamonix offers. It's certainly worth a winter. You can buy a ski pass for about $1,200 that gives you access to six different ski mountains and a bus pass. Within minutes, the high-tech tram system whisks you from town, at 3,842 feet, to summits as high as 12,650 feet. Boundless off-piste and backcountry opportunities are legally accessible from where the tram drops you off—a benefit and freedom that skiers and mountaineers in the States can only dream about.

Each morning you can choose a new adventure—for example, at the Grands Montets (literally, "big little mountains"). With a lift system rising 9,000 feet from the valley floor, the Grands Montets complex is immense, with runs ranging from steep chutes to incredibly wide, long bowls. Skiing "tram laps" is unrivaled by anything in the States—you can ski fast, non-stop, for half an hour at a time. The vistas of the surrounding mountains and glaciers are breathtaking.

A don't-miss adventure is the day-long journey down one of the many runs accessible from atop the Aiguille du Midi (Needle of the South), the king of Chamonix's ski mountains. Unless you're an expert at glacier travel, you'll need to hire a guide to keep you out of the crevasses on the Mer de Glace (Sea of Ice). The Aiguille du Midi is a wonderful introduction to raid français (French backcountry).

A trip to Chamonix remains incomplete without the quintessential intermediate ski down the Vallée Blanche, a beautiful, easy day-trip which winds through a labyrinth of crevasses 17 miles long. For more excitement and a greater challenge, we found superb snow on the steep and exposed Glacier Rhône, another well-known, full-day ski off the Aiguille du Midi. Since it's a 10,000-foot vertical descent from the top to town, you'll be well advised to pack a picnic of fresh baguettes et fromages. You'll find a boulangerie on almost every corner in town, and there's no such thing as old, cold bread.

The extensive backcountry hut system, which traverses into Switzerland and Italy, makes multi-day ski trips comfortable and convenient. We had an unforgettable experience summitting and skiing the Aiguille du Chardonnay, 12,600 feet high. A quick tram ride to the top of the Grands Montets, followed by a day of skinning, was all it took to reach an alpine hut at the foot of the climb.

You can't summarize Chamonix easily. It's the mountains, the food, the wine, the cozy farmhouses and chalets tucked away in beautiful valleys and hidden by flowers, the history of alpinism, the vast verticals. Every expert skier deserves a trip there to discover the magic first hand. C'est si bon.

Nobody makes a baguette like the French. Rob and the Greek (Dean Decas) outside the bakery between runs on the Auguille du Midi.

It's hard to get an idea of scale in big mountains. See the glacier down there? That's a good 2,000 feet below Rob as he sweeps a turn off the Pas de Chèvre sets up to ski into the Couloir Rectiligne.

of snow safety principles, your common sense, and your cautious attitude.

Avalanche hazard depends on snow history, current weather, and the steepness of the slope. New-fallen snow will slide more often than old snow will. New snow doesn't come just from the clouds—it can also be deposited by the wind. Warm sun, or simply warm temperatures, will make the snow heavier and more likely to slide. In 1996, Canadian Trevor Peterson, an experienced mountaineer and extreme skier, was killed in Chamonix in a couloir supposedly by an avalanche that occurred in the late afternoon on a sunny day. The safest snow in a couloir is spring corn snow—stable but easy to set an edge in and soft enough to slow your slide if you should fall.

In a place like Chamonix, you also need to know where you are going. Because the area comprises hundreds of square miles of lift-serviced terrain, much of it poorly marked, you could easily ski down a couloir that ends in a cliff. It's sometimes possible to follow others who seem to know where they're going—but if you don't want to be led into terrain you can't handle, you had better be their skiing equal or better. A couloir is no place to go off exploring blindly. That's why, despite our background, we asked our friend Alex Fandel to lead the way, and why even expert skiers should hire an experienced guide.

In France, it's also important to buy the Carte Neige mountain-rescue insurance policy. It costs about $35 for a year's coverage and is definitely worth it. Helicopter rescue services are available, and are very efficient. But they're also very expensive. Carte Neige ("snow card") will cover your rescue bill.

LEAVE THE ROPES

In one of the more memorable scenes from Greg Stump's classic late-'80s ski film The Blizzard of Aahhhs, extreme skiers Scot Schmidt, Glen Plake and Mike Hattrup rappel over a cliff to reach a famous line above Chamonix, France, called Couloir Poubelle—in English, "the garbage chute." It's a place of towering rock walls, awesome steeps and epic snow. Scot's understated comments, over the inspiring shots from Glen's helmet camera, made this couloir look like the kind of big-time extreme skiing we relish. We couldn't wait to get there.

We don't need no stinking rope. Well…

Nearly 10 years later, we're in the parking lot of the Grands Montets Téléphérique, just up-valley from Chamonix, with ski buddies Dean Decas, Kristen Lignell, and Kristen Ulmer. The anticipation is killing us. We joke about those great scenes from the film with our friend and unofficial tour guide, Alex Fandel. He smiles as if he knows something we don't. A tram and a gondola ride later, we're peering over the flimsy cable fence that guards the entrance to the Poubelle itself. Below us a thin mist shrouds the couloir and the huge rock walls edging it. We barely contain our excitement at the thought of lowering ourselves into this abyss, with all our cool climbing gear, to reenact the movie.

The wind shifts, the mist disappears, and we're rewarded with our first view of the glacial floor 5,000 feet below. Suddenly there is a scuttling sound behind us. A crowd of French skiers push past us, practically vault over the cable, and disappear over the edge. No ropes. No harnesses. No climbing gear. We gape in wonder. A religious cult on a suicide mission?

Then we look over the edge—and laugh. Alex, enjoying the joke, points out the spot where Scot, Glen, and Mike made their totally unnecessary rappel, purely for cinematic effect. Most skiers simply climb down over the low-angled rock face below us, holding onto the fixed-but-fraying rope for support. The French, like the group just ahead of us, do this nonchalantly—it's no big deal. The couloir runs about 42 degrees of pitch—that's steep, but it's not life-threatening even with those 100-foot rock buttresses on either side. Those Frenchmen weren't on a suicide mission—they were just powderhounds intent on beating us to first tracks.

Chuckling with a combination of relief and embarrassment, we jump in after the French party and begin our first Chamonix couloir experience down a slot manageable by anyone with some basic grasp of steep-skiing technique. It's great fun, and, in fact, turns out to be a perfect introduction to Cham's many incredible couloirs, just because it's so easily accessible.

You don't need to read French to understand what these signs say. It is not uncommon in Cham to see people riding the lifts with backpacks, ice-axes and crampons.

Skiing the Garbage Chute

Even before reaching the Couloir Poubelle, we had gathered the following facts to use in our assessment of its safety: It had been snowing off and on for the past four days. The new snow, about 10 to 12 inches, definitely had slide potential. However, there had been very little temperature fluctuation during the storm, so we expected that the snow crystals had bonded together well. Before this storm, the snowpack had been very stable, another good sign.

The day was calm, with no signs of wind effects on the snow—there had been no visible loading, striping, or slabbing. It was also quite cold at the top, so the snow should have stayed light, which is always good for stability. But the sun was supposed to come out as the afternoon progressed, and since the Poubelle Couloir faces the afternoon sun, that could be a problem. And it was going to be quite a bit warmer at the bottom of the couloir than at the top. We decided to drop in before the sun had a chance to warm the snow.

The technique for skiing any couloir is dictated by its steepness, width and the quality of the snow, which can change as you descend. The obvious goal is to make controlled turns and stay safe. All steep techniques stem from the fundamental pedal turn, in which you step off the uphill ski, pull the downhill ski up aggressively, and pivot it in the direction of the new turn. The momentum of this action pulls the uphill ski up and out of the snow, and you start your new turn in the air. When the snow is light, the couloir wide, or the slope less steep, you can keep your skis on the snow through part of the

Eric makes a turn coming into the crux of the Couloir des Poubelles. It's bigger than it looks...see Rob way down by the rocks?

Stay on your skis and finish each in balance before going into your next one. In Chamonix and other areas that offer truly big, radical skiing, you can't let your desire to accomplish a specific goal override your ability to handle it.

turn, and that saves energy. This is key for long descents when you're wearing a heavy pack.

Once we got down into the Poubelle, we found that the rocks walls were even higher than they looked from above—absolutely awesome. In the throat at the top, the couloir is only about 10 feet wide, but down toward the middle it widens to at least 60 feet. The snow was deeper than we expected, and quite heavy. Because of the steepness and width at the top, typical medium-radius powder technique wouldn't work. The only feasible way to ski this was to use powerful pedal turns to get our skis up and out of the heavy boot-deep powder.

As we descended, the sun grew hotter and the snow heavier but less deep. The pitch mellowed to about 35 degrees. Skier traffic also grew heavier. Popular place, this Garbage

Chute. Midway down, where the couloir opens up, all the crisscrossing tracks from other skiers had broken up the new snow. Here we found another variation of the pedal turn to be most effective: a fall line version using a narrower stance and less pivoting in the air. By keeping our skis closer together at the bottom of the turn, we could prevent them from sinking too deeply into the heavy snow, which made it easier to start the next turn. We still pedaled the downhill leg up to initiate the turn in the air, but it was unnecessary to pivot the skis so far around while airborne. Minimizing the up-action was far less tiring.

We still had about 1,000 vertical feet to go. The sun had heated the surrounding rock walls, softening the new snow clinging to them and sending wet white clods cascading into the

This line was not what Rob expected. It would have been a good idea to hike it first. The numbers refer to the photos on the next two pages.

couloir. This was potentially a dangerous situation, especially if the snow should bring loose rocks with it. It was time to get going, so we picked up the pace.

Once out from between the rock walls, we made a long traverse to a beautiful lunch spot with a perfect view back up the couloir. In the afternoon, we skied one final powder-laden face below Les Drus, the famous granite spires above the Vallée Blanche. Then we descended the glacier and followed the cat track into town. Our single run had taken most of the day. We hadn't cheated death at all. We just had a great day of low-risk couloir fun.

Over the next two weeks we would explore the countless couloirs of Chamonix, testing our own limits and living a reality far more incredible than anything we'd seen on film.

Hike it first

If you drop into a blind couloir, sometimes conditions aren't what you expect. You may find ice, for example. And ice on a super-steep slope is deadly.

Several days after our Poubelle experience, we stood looking at an enticing couloir. It had no name, and from across the bowl, looked steep and narrow—a classic line. It appeared that the snow had slid, which usually creates an icy surface in the slide path. But it was getting direct sun, so the snow might have softened up. It seemed worth a closer look.

From the top, we were surprised to see that the couloir dropped over a roll and out of sight after about eight turns worth of slope. The snow in the entry looked stable. Rob volunteered to check it out.

He dropped in, and the shadowed face where he landed was steeper than expected. The

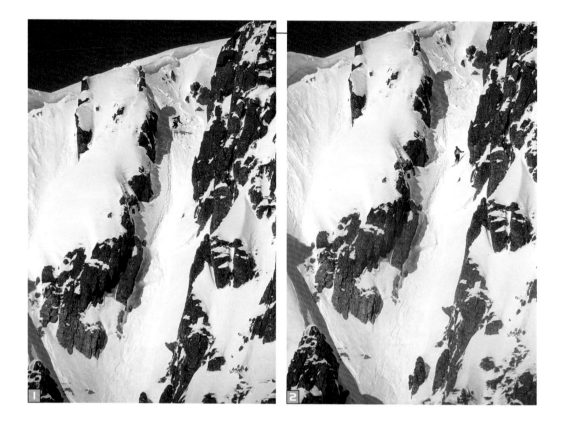

surface layer of snow slid under his skis but left him standing in boot-deep powder. From the brink of the drop-off, he had his first look at the whole couloir, and he didn't like what he saw: Previous slides had carved a concave trough right down the middle (photos above). A concave surface is tenuous because it is difficult or impossible to get the whole ski edge on the snow for grip when your skis are across the hill. Also, the trough would make it easy to catch a tip or tail in a hop turn.

Rob sidestepped down the narrow 55-degree slope, made one turn—and landed on ice. He thought, "If I hop a turn, will my edges hold? When was the last time I tuned my skis? Could I get my skis off and climb up or down on this ice?" He considered running it straight, the entire length. But it was a long way, over 1,000

feet, and the tightest section was a snow ditch. At very high speed, one mistake would carry him straight into the cliff wall. He breathed deeply, sidestepped down a little further, made another turn (photo 3). His edges held. By minimizing the hop in the turn, he found he could settle into each new turn gently, and hold the edge.

The pitch mellowed a little nearing the tight exit zone. The couloir was shaped like a funnel, but with that ditch in the middle. Rob set his edges by hopping from one bank of the ditch to the other until it got too narrow. He stopped to assess the situation.

Rob was stuck in the throat of the exit, which was narrower than his skis were long (photo 4). The trough here was two feet deep and very steep. Hanging by the tips and tails of his

A run like this will not always be pretty to ski, but a fall would be even less attractive. Sometimes you just have to do what it takes to get down safely.

skis, he contemplated a straight run to the bottom, now not far below. But the open bowl beyond appeared to be covered with crusty snow and refrozen slide debris—not a healthy place to tumble. He took a few deep breaths for focus and sidestepped down. Gingerly. Finally, as the funnel opened up, he found room to turn beside the ditch (photo 5).

Connecting turns never felt so refreshing. With relief, Rob coasted across the bowl toward Eric, who had descended via another route to wait. We had learned something: Always hike an unknown couloir before you ski it. Just as balance and control are the keys to safety, patience and conservative choices may be the keys to survival.

The Mental Game

There's no question that skiing steep slopes is mentally challenging. If someone tells either of us that he has never been scared by a radical steep line, then we know we're talking to someone who has not skied an extremely steep slope. Everybody who has truly challenged himself has had to conquer fear at some level. It is the ability to overcome fear and rise to the challenge that separates average skiers from great skiers.

For many, many talented skiers, it is hard to maintain their normally strong technique when they are skiing a steep, challenging descent. The brain kicks in too much in this per-

There is no line steeper and faster than this one. Adam (right) and Rob airing it out. Location: above the Argentiere Glacier, Chamonix.

ceived dangerous environment (whether real or imagined) and inhibits the ability of the skier to perform up to his or her normal level.

Many skiers who are advancing to the steeps experience a "cycle of fear" followed by a realization of the true nature of the challenge, and then finally acceptance of the situation. This doesn't happen all the time, but we have seen it enough to bring it up here in hopes that you may avoid the inherent pitfalls it can present. Some people have the ability to adapt naturally to challenge and to perform as needed. But for many, many people here is how it goes.

The first stage generally occurs when the skier goes through a dramatic improvement in ability and suddenly feels invincible and ready for fresh challenges. The problem arises when the skier's newfound skills exceed his or her ability to recognize and evaluate the existing hazards of a given run. Often there's not even a sense of the real danger until something happens. Usually there is some kind of eye-opening experience, a wakeup call. For example, we have a client who is a really strong skier, but who, on one occasion, hadn't seen the whole picture.

Eric tells the story: "We were heli-skiing in Alaska. Deano and I were skiing with this client in a really steep, cool zone that can best be described as chute-like ramps of snow at about 48 degrees. Good and steep. The snow was really sweet, knee-deep powder, so the threat of a slide-for-life was low. Everybody felt really excited about this slope. It had a dual fall line where, if you drifted left, you could ski an aspect that you could not see as you skied the regular part of the run. Our heli guide, Dean Cummings, pointed this out very clearly to all of us before anyone skied down. Unfortunately, "Mr. Happy" did not process this information, because he was so amped up to go first. Down low in the chute, he took a hard left (just what he was warned against doing) and flew off a 35-foot cliff which, by pure luck, landed him safely onto the glacier below. He was fine, despite his fine effort to the contrary, and he told me later that he went off without knowing it was there and that upon the realization that he was flying through the air, he made a noise that he had never made in his life! The moral of the story: You have to keep your wits about you and be mindful of the mountain, because the mountain is not conscious of you, little people that we are."

The next stage of the fear and reality cycle occurs usually after something dramatic or life threatening happens, either to oneself or to a skiing companion (typically a serious fall). The result: serious jitters on the steeps and being really scared for no good reason. This is also a vulnerable stage, because the person gets so wound up and scared, his or her natural ability to ski well flies out the window. This is just as dangerous as overconfidence, because it is really hard to ski well when the brain is fried and the body is tensed. Occasionally we have seen someone fall over while standing still, because they were so nervous.

The bottom line: You need to ski enough in unexposed steep zones to become comfortable with steeps and familiar with the process of recognizing, evaluating and becoming comfortable with the inherent risks. It is always best to be conservative. Learn to nurture and trust your intuition through the evolutionary process of skiing steep terrain. It's a progression, a learning process. Over time you want to train the brain to balance ability and desire with the realities of the mountain environment.

Learning, training and controlling the mental aspects of steep skiing can be done. Here are some thoughts on how you can accomplish this safely:

Getting into the steeps takes a lot of days on the hill. Start with short steep runs, with no real danger in the event of a fall. The run can be very steep, but it should be very short and have a safe run-out so that, if you fall, you can slide to the bottom without having to worry about hitting a tree or flying off a cliff. Before

Between runs and heading up for more. Left to right: Dean Decas, Eric, Rob and Matt Herrigger. Chamonix, 1996.

you go, take a good look at the slope you're going to ski. Take a deep breath and visualize (if you can) your run to come. Feel yourself on the slope before you even put a ski on it. Take another deep breath and get ready to go.

It is okay to sideslip. One time our friend Matty Moo (far right in photo above) was skiing the Whymper Couloir in Chamonix with Rob. Rob had skied down a ways and was waiting for Matty. Matty eased onto the slope, was a little nervous (as he should have been) and, with a smile, asked Rob: "Is it okay to sideslide here?" Yes, it's always okay! Sideslipping gives you a good feel for the slope and builds a level of security, but remember that you always have to be on your skis. Do not lean into the slope, or you'll be in for trouble, even when just sideslipping.

As you ski down, maintain constant awareness of the many factors influencing your evolving and spontaneous choices of turn style, speed, and line selection. Feel your skis on the snow. Feel the snow under your skis. Be conscious. Be aware. Be mindful of the mountain. As you become more comfortable, progress to longer and steeper runs. As you do so, you will become more familiar with yourself, your abilities and the steep environment itself.

Longevity and good times on steep terrain are grounded in The Decision. Know when to go. Know when to walk away. You have to be in the moment and know that if you do not feel good about a certain run, you do not have to ski it today. The same run will be there the next day or the next year.

Nurturing your experience nurtures your intuition. Your intuition is your guardian angel. You have to learn to trust your feelings and become comfortable with the relationship between yourself and the mountain. We have all had days where, for some unexplained reason, we have had bad feelings about a run for no good reason other then "it just didn't feel right." In just about every case, especially where there were obvious hazards, we each have walked away. More often then not, we returned later to ski it succesfully. There will always be times when you should walk away. The alternative may not be pretty.

Take your time to nurture your intuition and improve your ability in the steeps, and you will learn to ski and enjoy them safely and thoroughly with the respect they deserve. As you progress down these steep slopes, your opportunities become endless for seeking the challenges and rewards of skiing the whole mountain.

Our friend Kristen Lignell enjoying herself in the late afternoon sunshine.

Whether in the East or the West, tree skiing offers good snow and endless options.

chapter 5

MOGULS AND TREES

East is East and West is West.

We all know that skiing in the West is very different from skiing in the East. The elevations are much higher in the West, which means the snow is drier. Much of good skiing lies above timberline, in open bowls and on exposed ridges.

By contrast, the mountains of the Northeast are very old. Over a billion years old, the Adirondacks are the oldest mountains on earth, about three times the age of the oldest dinosaurs. The range has been pushed up twice. After the first uplift, its peaks may have been over 30,000 feet high, higher than Everest. The second time, the Adirondacks were about the height of today's Rockies. They've had about 500 million years to erode to their present stature. Which is uniformly below timberline.

The Green Mountains of Vermont, our home state, do not exceed 4,500 feet in elevation. There's no timberline: Trees run from bottom to top. The ski runs are carved right out of the forest, and they're fairly narrow. This concentrates skier traffic, so the steeper runs get bumped up quickly. To be an expert skier in the East means being a great mogul skier.

Because the trails are narrow, you head for the woods if you want a lot of skiable acreage. Tree skiing in the Northeast is tough, uncompromising and absolutely grand. The dense woods often harbor stashes of fresh snow. But it's not the bottomless powder of the West, so when you ski Eastern trees, you encounter stumps, bumps, small waterfall, nasty little cliffs and frozen creek beds. Most of the time, the snow surface is firm or frozen.

Eastern bump and tree skiing requires the sharpest of all-mountain skiing technique. It demands honed edging skills, finely tuned balance, agility and the mental awareness to look ahead. Ski well in the Northeast, and you can ski well anywhere.

In the West, a much larger percentage of the ski terrain is above the tree line. Lifts provide access to more skiable acreage. Open

Mogul skiing under a chairlift is always a crowd pleaser, as Adam DesLauriers and Gabbie Valasquez demonstrate beneath lift 4 at Bolton Valley, Vermont.

By its very nature, tree skiing requires both mogul skiing skills and the ability to look ahead and adjust on the fly. Skiers: Adam DesLauriers and Dean Decas. Location: Bolton Valley.

Left: Eric vaporizes a powdery mogul at Sun Valley, Idaho. Below: Bigger trees do not always mean more space to ski between them.

bowls and chutes invite us to explore the high alpine environment. At lower elevations, below the tree line, the skiing terrain is defined, with groomed runs cut through the trees. This is much more like Eastern skiing, but with wide, sweeping runs. Off the cut trails, the trees are often larger and more widely spaced—the skier has more space, and more time, to plan a line through the trees than in the East.

Of course, there are exceptions. In Telluride and Crested Butte, for instance, the tree skiing is every bit as tight and gnarly as in the East, and in the temperate rainforest of Whistler-Blackcomb, below 5,000 feet, the woods are impassable even to summer hikers. In general, though, Western areas show us long, broad faces with softer snow, and the tree skiing here is simply more friendly.

Mogul skiing is pretty consistent from coast to coast. The big difference is the solidity of the surface. Eastern bump skiing makes you tough as nails, while Western bump skiing, on softer snow, can spoil a skier. It lets you get away with less precise technique. This is not to say that the skiers are less hardy. It is just that you tend to fall less often, and it hurts less when you do.

Mogul and tree technique

Skiing well in moguls requires specific application of the same skills we have been covering so far in this book. You need a low stance, strong edging, good timing and proactive movement of the legs and feet to maintain snow contact over the undulating terrain of the mogul field. The legs pump and move under the upper body. The

BOLTON VALLEY GOES TO SQUAW

Growing up at Bolton Valley, when we were not racing gates, we skied bumps. This combination was great for our skiing. We tore it up under Lift 4, on a trail very appropriately named Show Off. It was here that we and our friends jokingly thrived on the cheers of the crowd. And the springtime bump contest was always a blast. The first competition was held when we were just 11 and 10 years old, respectively. It's tough to remember who, exactly, took home more first place trophies. But it was always a blast.

This early bumping paid of in all sorts of ways. When Eric arrived in Squaw Valley in '87 at the tail end of a two-month road trip touring and skiing the West, he entered a pro mogul contest on his last bottom dollar. He pulled off an upset and placed fifth overall. The $500 prize money extended his Squaw stay for another week of awesome spring skiing. So awesome that both of us ended up moving to Squaw Valley the very next season and the rest is history!

upper body must hold position squarely over the feet. Shoulders and hands must, at all times, face down the hill toward the next turn.

Tree skiing is largely about tactics—how you look ahead and ski your line. The turn radius, and therefore the technique, of tree skiing is dictated primarily by the spacing of the trees and the pitch of the hill. Your personal style may lead you to take a faster or slower line. But the basic moves derive from the same simple, solid all-mountain technique we've described in the previous chapters.

In this chapter, we will cover mogul skiing technique, and we will detail some tactics and tricks to help you in the trees. It is safe to say that, East or West, all good skiers should be able to hold it together in moguls, and be able to lay down good tracks in trees.

Mogul skiing

Skiing moguls is great fun—and the cornerstone of expert-level steep skiing at Eastern resorts. Even the trees skiing spots bump up quickly because of the crowds—how often have you seen an Eastern glade consisting of bumps with trees everywhere between them? "Moguls" or "bumps" can describe anything from long whale-backs to mini-mountains the shape and size of Volkswagen Beetles to chattery, square-sided hay bales to narrow chutes with only one serpentine path through them.

Our preferred technique is not the FIS World Cup style you see Jonny Moseley and other competitive bumpers using in the Olympics. That technique is a high speed sprint, in which the skis skip off the sides and tops of the bumps. It works in the perfectly crafted bump courses of the competition circuit. If you want to ski bumps like this, you should look up ex-world champion Nelson Carmichael in Steamboat Springs, and sign up for his mogul skiing camp. We don't teach it, because it doesn't work so well at speeds less then 40 mph or for normal humans in the real world of unpredictable, oddly shaped moguls, multiple fall lines and changing pitch steepness.

Instead, we encourage a no-nonsense

Absorbing a stumpy bump in the trees. Dean makes it look easy by picking his feet up before clearing the lip in order to get his skis back on the snow and into his next turn as quickly as possible.

style of bump skiing based on carving your turns. This style of bump skiing is versatile and strong, and it will work regardless of pitch, mogul size or snow conditions. Whether you ski big soft bumps or nasty icy bumps, this technique will have you shredding them in no time. The technique itself builds off everything we have covered so far. The goal is to maximize your efficiency, control, and flowing balance while bumping your way down the hill. The technique described below works for all short radius turns in any bumpy conditions, even crud or other off-piste variable snow.

The essentials of all mountain skiing apply. You need to focus on:

- Photo 1: Applying strong edging and focusing your energy.
- Photo 2: Using a good stance and allowing absorption with the legs.
- Photo 3: Relaxing to release each turn while retracting the legs.
- Photo 4: Leading the edge change with the inside foot light and tipping to the little-toe side as the skis clear the bump.
- Photo 5: Extending the legs after the crest of the bump to maximize snow contact in the trough.
- Photo 6: Looking far down the hill to find a

In Photo 4, you can clearly see Kit leading her edge change with her new inside foot, keeping it light and tipping to her little-toe edge. In Photo 5, her feet are at matching edge angles, and she is just starting her new turn onto the bump below. In Photo 6 she in perfect position to absorb the next bump. Notice how her hands are always out in front, leading the way down the hill.

smooth, non-confrontational line through the bumps.

Because you have been working on these techniques on groomed and natural snow, it should be relatively easy to apply them to moguls. When you do, you should feel a smooth rhythm, a good link between turns and an encouraging level of balance and control.

Choosing a line

First, let's define some terms. The face of the mogul is the side you see first, the uphill side facing the oncoming skier. The back of the mogul is the side facing downhill. The objective is not to go straight over the tops of the bumps, but to carve the sides and backs. Turn completion happens using the face of the bump as a speed control bank, and the transition happens between the bumps.

Speed control is essential in the bumps. To soften the impact with the front of the next bump, control your speed on each turn with the shave-and-soft-turn completion move you learned to use in crud snow.

As you carve around the side and over the back of one bump, you should carve your turn completion into the next mogul at about a 45-degree angle from above. To do this, you need a good stance, with the skis parallel. This is like the bottom of a turn, except that you anticipate an impact when you hit the bump. It's easier to ski smoothly in soft-snow bumps for two reasons: 1) the soft surface makes it easier to feather your edges for speed control, so you meet the next bump with less energy; and 2) the face of the bump itself is softer, a bit more cushioned.

Hard-snow bumps are another story. Here, you need a much more aggressive speed control move. You have to get more edge bite on each bump. The trick is to make a quick, efficient, balanced edge set—and release it quickly to keep your momentum moving down the hill. Keep your eyes, hands and shoulders centered squarely over the feet and facing the next turn in your chosen line.

You need that quick edge set to control your speed. As soon as you set your edges, plant your downhill pole for timing. Quickly absorb the energy, and the bump, by drawing your legs up into your stomach. Flow over the contours of the bump and extend your legs to maintain edge contact down the back of the bump. Use this mantra: set, plant, absorb, flow.

As your legs absorb up into your body, the key move is to make your edge change as quickly as possible. Always lead the edge change move with the new inside foot.

Be patient and let the bump come to you. Be ready for the next bump. Stay low and relaxed, poised for the impact. As your ski tips hit the bump, begin to absorb (retract your knees and legs) early to lessen the impact. Repeat as needed.

Once you get the rhythm and movement down, you will find that this bump skiing style has a lot of application for skiing the whole mountain when you are forced to use short-radius turns. Especially in high-traffic areas of the mountain, you will find chutes and glades chock-full of bumps. Because of this, you'll find these bumper-type turns very effective when skiing in chutes and trees as well.

Tree skiing
Tree skiing is terrific off-piste fun, and it is available at almost every resort in the country. More and more ski resorts are opening up tree skiing areas, especially in the East. The trees

BILL'S BUMP TIPS

1. Always keep your hands out in front of your body where you can see them in your peripheral vision. Think of reaching down the hill with your hands.
2. Use your pole plants to set your rhythm. Plant your pole a moment sooner then you think you should, just as your ski tips hit the next bump. Reach downhill to make the pole plant.
3. Never lose shin contact with your boot tongues.
4. As you clear each bump, actively push your feet down into the troughs to maintain snow contact as you approach the next bump.
5. In some cases, forget about route-finding through the bumps and simply keep making short-radius turns regardless of where the bumps are.
6. Mix up your turn radii. Try making medium-radius turns from time to time, then short-radius turns, then back to medium turns.

As the popularity of skiing off groomed runs increases, resorts are making tree-skiing glades more accessible.

are also where you're most likely to find freshies after a storm.

Skiing well in the forest depends on developing your tactical awareness and planning on the move. You have to look for the open spaces. Focus on the white between the trees and don't be distracted by the trees whizzing by as you ski down the hill. Imagine staring at every oncoming car on a two-lane road: Sooner or later you'd hit one for sure. When you're driving a car, the trick is to simply look ahead at the pavement in your own lane, and relax. It's exactly the same in tree skiing. Look at your intended route, not at the trees themselves. Trees are like visual magnets; if you look at them directly, they draw you towards them, so look at the spaces between them, right where you want to go.

Because trees do not grow in a set pattern, your line options are endless. In your favor is the fact that many people tend to follow existing tracks. This creates a "rut line," and by avoiding it you can often find better snow. By being flexible yet precise with your line, you can usually find a nice rhythm in the tightest of trees. Line choice, looking ahead, turn radius, and the placement of your edge set all blend together so when you really nail a good run it's amazing. Your best runs seem easy.

To ski the trees fluidly, you need confidence in your ability and some tactical rules. Specifically:

• Most important, **ski with a buddy**. If something goes wrong, you want to have someone to help you out. If something goes really wrong, you want someone to tell the ski patrol.

Expert foresters Adam DesLauriers and Dean Decas take a run among mixed yellow and white birch and small evergreens.

Trees are like visual magnets: If you look at them, they draw you in like the Death Star tractor beam. So look at the gaps between the trees. Or look for the light (left). Darkness ahead (below) should be avoided. Light is good, darkness is trouble.

What can go wrong? You can land in a tree well—eventually everyone does. Our partner, Dean Decas, fell into one and almost lost consciousness before his tree-skiing buddy dug his head out. So, even the best can get into trouble on a bad day. So, ski with a friend in the trees. It's safer then skiing alone and more fun anyway.

• As we said above (but it's worth repeating), the absolute Golden Rule of skiing in the trees is this: **Look at the gaps** between the trees, not at the trees themselves. Look where you want to go. Be aware of the forest but do not look right at the trees.

• **Look for the light** and ski there; ski to the light. If you look ahead and see light around or just beyond a tree or stand of trees, then chances are good you can keep going and make at least another turn. If you see nothing but darkness in the trees, you may be looking at jail time. Quickly consider an alternative line.

• Think about your **turn placement.** Usually you want to turn above and below the trees, not right next to a tree. If you think about it, you are skinniest when your skis are pointed straight down the hill. So set up your move through tight spots by placing a turn right above

Facing page: This sequence shows a good turn placement to shoot the gap between two large trees. Eyes and shoulders are always facing where you want to go. In Photos 2 and 3, Eric lays down the turn so that his edge set (finish of the turn) is right above the tree he will go around. He then releases the turn (Photo 4) and sets up to turn through the gap (Photos 5 and 6). You should set up your turn so that you are lined up vertically over your feet as you go through the narrowest part. **Right:** Adam puts it all together.

the tight section. Turn into the fall line through the tight passage, and exit into the open as you complete your turn.

• Where it's really tight, be very precise about **turn placement.** Instead of thinking about the whole turn, think about where your boots are going to travel. Also, use every bit of space available: "Widen" the tight slot by turning your ski tails into the little alcoves in the trees.

• **Control your speed** in the trees with more turns, rather than fewer.

• **Be ready to hit the brakes.** You will, without a doubt, encounter unexpected obstacles (downed trees, cliffs, streambeds), so ski at a speed that allows you to stop right now, or at least bail out. Stopping is your only for-sure bet to avoid trouble, so ski at a speed where you can do this on very short notice.

• **Know your foliage.** In the East, tree skiing means hardwood (bare trunks), ever-

greens (trunks protected by tenting branches), or, near streams, pucker brush. Where it's tight, you can generally bull through the branches of the evergreens and plow through any pucker brush that is one inch or less in diameter. Just wear your goggles and let it rip. In the West, you'll encounter alders and aspen near streams and marshy meadows. The same one-inch rule holds true here. But the evergreens are different in the West. The branches are thicker, often as strong as the trunk of an Eastern pine, and whip tough. If you try to push through, you'll bounce off, or be clotheslined like a quarterback getting hit by a linebacker! Get knocked over by one these bad-boys and you may wind up gasping for breath and upside in its tree well.

Finally, as our great friend and ski partner Dean Decas loves to say: "Have fun out there. And keep both skis on the same side of the tree!"

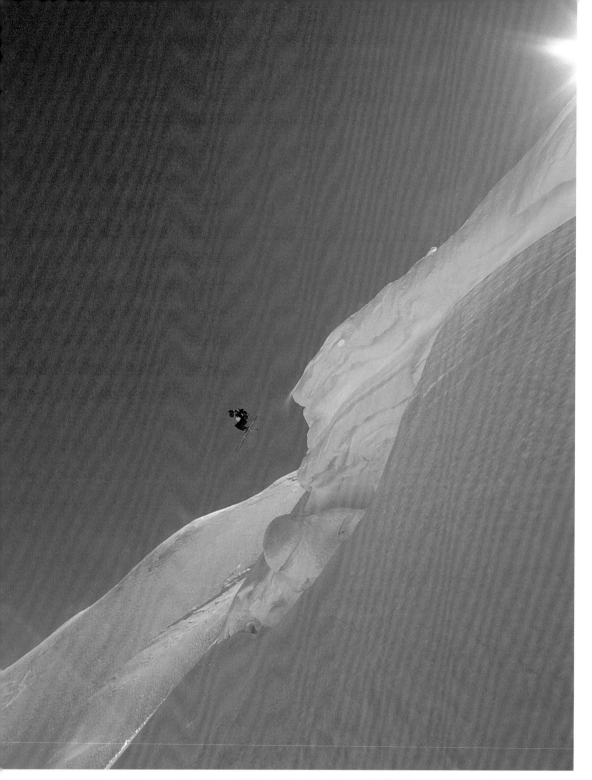

Catching air is a great rush—and it's not that hard to pull off. Airman: Rob DesLauriers.

chapter 6

AIR AND OTHER SECRETS

Skiing the whole mountain is more than perfect turns. Here are a few cool moves that will have you leaving tracks in some very cool places.

Skiing is an endless learning curve, challenging the mind and body with a new and fresh run every time we head down the hill. The better you get at skiing, the more options—and challenges—the mountains will present to you.

As you gain this experience, you find many little tricks and secrets—what we call skiing savvy. Most air, for example, isn't so much a specialized technique as it is a collection of little bits of knowledge applied to a variety of situations. Launching air safely and efficiently in a ski run is often quite simple and is a matter of good judgment, timing, body position and fluid movement.

When you ski well, you can begin to push past your self-imposed limits to experience the freedom of skiing the whole mountain, to confidently apply your skills to the endless variety of terrain the mountains offer. In this chapter, we will present a variety of situations. All of them, including air-time, can be handled with the movements we have been covering in the previous chapters. We will apply these essential movements of sound skiing (relax to release the turn, patiently flow through transition and lead the edge change with the lightened inside foot, letting the skis, not muscle power, engage the new turn) to unique situations, the kind you will see more and more frequently in your own skiing as you ski more miles and range farther out to get the goods.

We will also discuss a few topics relating to more general skiing savvy to help you gain a well-rounded repertoire of skills (a few different arrows for your quiver, so to speak), to negotiate the mountains with poise, confidence and style.

As you read through these, take note of the simplicity and consistency of the essential movements as they apply to each example. Try not to confuse things by getting too technical. Look for simplicity and the continuity that exists by melding uncomplicated technique with modern skis. It is the continuity of sound skiing skills, which can be applied time and time again in wide ranging snow conditions and terrain challenges. Stay true to form and maintain the focus to apply your fundamental technique to these examples and you will exceed your expectations and expand your capabilities. Then get out and go!

Flow like water

To ski as water flows is one of our great ambitions. How does a stream of water flow over and around an obstacle? Imagine a fat raindrop coursing down a rough roof. Upon meeting an obstacle—a nailhead, say—the leading edge of the drop stops. The body of the drop compresses. Then, ever so smoothly, the leading edge finds the path of least resistance around the nailhead, and flows forward again as the droplet decompresses. Your skis and feet are that leading edge, and your whole skiing self is that raindrop.

Don't be scared of a steep pitch just because it's steep. Look at the slope and decide what would happen if you fall. If there is nothing (no rocks or lift towers, for example) to hurt you, then no problem. Focus on what you're doing and ski it.

Photo 1: Casually flowing down the mountain, our raindrop du jour is Eric. Our obstacle is a shallow cornice precipice.

Photo 2: A thinking and skilled raindrop, he approaches with a well placed turn so as to cushion his impact and thus avoid splashing uncontrollably.

Photo 3: Eric is beginning to compress on the true front of the obstacle. His skis and feet—his leading edge—have slowed by crossing the fall line. With skis almost stalled, the rest of his body is still moving forward as it compresses down against his leading edge. This continued flow by his body keeps his critical momentum going.

His hips compress towards his heels, shoulders over his leading ski edge and facing down the fall line. He is ready to flow.

Photo 4: Without hesitation, his skis release along the path of least resistance, flowing down the fall line as his body decompresses. Speed controlled, raindrop intact, Eric's nearly imperceptible actions lead to gracious fluidity . . . as water flows.

Corkscrew air turn

One of the most thrilling things you can do on skis is to launch confidently into a clean air, and land smoothly into the next turn. The basic technique and footwork is consistent with the moves we've been building. Now you can take them off a safe cliff, landing and skiing into your dreams.

In this photo sequence, Eric is skiing confidently into a clean air off a cliff, airplaning the transition and floating cleanly to a perfect landing

Photo 1: Eric finishes his set-up turn, perfectly placed for smooth flow off the cliff. The skis are evenly weighted and at matching edge angles. He's balanced on the balls of his feet, right in the middle of the skis. The upper body and eyes are focused right at the chosen landing spot. He is compressed and balanced— poised to release the turn and uncoil for the transition off the drop. This compact, compressed stance is great in steep terrain like this, and provides the additional benefit of minimizing the airtime of your torso. Downhill racers make this same absorption move before every jump— coaches often call the move a pre-jump.

Photo 2: To release this turn and flow off the drop, Eric confidently relaxes his downhill leg, transferring his weight to the uphill ski and drawing his upper body downhill towards his landing spot. He lets go with his uphill leg as well. This draws the upper body across the skis and flattens them to the snow surface just as he is going off the drop. He retracts both legs slightly to lighten them for take-off. This is where you really have to maintain your composure. Focus on what you're doing. You can't rush

it or lean back. Eric is focused: He maintains a good stance over his skis, with toes, knees and shoulders lined up vertically.

Photo 3: The upper body is cranked toward the landing spot, providing the rotary torque to bring the legs and skis around in mid-flight to line up for landing. That landing is in the direction of the next turn. The body naturally unwinds in mid-air (photo 4), and the only thing you need to concentrate on is the new inside ski that is leading the edge change as the flight progresses. You must stay poised and patient. Notice the sound body position: Toes, knees, and shoulders are lined up, and eyes are focused on the landing spot. From here, the landing is piece of cake. The rest of the run is a whoop and a holler.

Tip 1: Coming into the drop, establish your turns with a tempo and turn radius which allows you to set your last turn in a spot above the take-off from which you can flow over the drop in the same cadence.

Tip 2: Your set-up and take off are everything. You have to manage your buzz of adrenaline. Stay focused and patient. Let the jump, the airtime and the landing come to you. Maintain your composure. You can handle this.

Progression into cliff airs

Skiers love air. Once you get it, you'll understand why. And it is worth loving; perhaps the greatest rush an expert skier ever gets is from a beautiful piece of air. But for many it's still a spectator sport. Air is about pointing it down the fall line, commitment, acceleration, speed and composure.

Set your turn above the notch so that you release it right before skiing through the notch.
Here Adam is hitting the turn with a firm edge set to control his speed.

Catching air is something you can actually evolve into with a controlled and systematic approach, minimizing the fear and pain of unintended landings. Break a good cliff drop down into its parts, practice each element in a separate and controlled way, then put it all back together.

Think about the parts: to catch air you will be freefalling down the fall line. You have to be totally committed to it, because once you point it off the cliff there is no bailing out. The acceleration is incredible, a very intense part of the overall rush. Then the sheer speed you achieve often makes the new air meister temporarily blind (which really makes the landing tricky). Yet, through it all you must maintain composure.

So how on earth (or slightly above it) does one acquire these skills? And that, my friends, is the question we are about to answer. You're skiing life may be changed forever, and it's as simple as one, two, three.

One: straightline the pitch next to the cliff you want to jump. Have you ever straight lined anything before? It's an incredible rush. You just point your skis down the fall line (photo 2) and don't bail out (photo 3). Holy *%#@! The acceleration, the speed, the commitment! Through it all maintain your composure. Check out photo 3; notice the balanced position, hands forward, upper body perpendicular to the slope, eyes and shoulders focused down the fall line. Repeat until you can maintain composure.

A good slope to practice air on will be steep enough to soften the landing but not so steep that if you take a fall you will pinwheel out of control. Also think about snow conditions. It's pretty simple: Soft snow is better than hard.

Two: straightline a sliver through the cliff band you want to jump (photo 1 and 2, at left). This often requires some sort of a small hop somewhere (photo 3) to get properly lined up for the exit. The sensations will be the same as straightlining next to the cliffs, but now there is a higher degree of commitment. Bailing out is simply not an option (photo 4). It's more intense, surrounded by rock, accelerating; it's almost like flying. Composure is key; repeat as needed until you are 100-percent comfortable.

Three: air it. Find a spot in you cliff with a clean take off (photo 1, at right), a comfortable size piece of air relative to your "warm up lines" (photo 2) with a clean steep landing (photo 3, next page). Point it and stay composed. Once you land it, you can control your speed by laying into some well-rounded, long-radius GS turns like we've talked about already. The double-top secret: the sensations will be the same as you felt in your straightlines; commitment, acceleration, speed and composure. Wow.

We often think about little kids skiing and how they want to go back time after time to the same jump or same little tree line. There is really something to learn here: work the same area until you complete the process. Just go for it. Commit to learning air and you can do it. Repetition and comfort are key. Be patient. Once you are successful in one area, you'll be amazed at how you can take your new skills elsewhere. It's a simple matter of evolution.

When in the air, never straighten out your body by reaching with your feet for your landing. Instead, keep your legs flexed and let the landing come to you, like Eric is doing here.

To use the pole push trick, you can't be going super fast or you will out-ski your ability to effectively push off with your poles.

Pole push trick

Now and then, you want to catch a little air but will need to clear some obstacle on take-off. Or you may want to launch a little higher in order to hit a pinpoint landing zone. The pole push trick is an energy-efficient way to generate a little extra loft. It also puts you into a good body position for the flight.

Photo 1: You are skiing toward the edge of a take-off zone. You set your turns to allow you to see the landing before you actually take off. When you see the landing, you realize the snow is thin. You wish you had more speed to reach a snow pillow four feet further on. But you're committed.

Photo 2: Plant both poles. Push down and back on the poles, lofting your upper body up and forward into the take off. Lift your knees and heels to get into a good flight position.

Photo 3 and 4: After you fly past your planted poles, and while your skis are floating towards your landing, turn your skis to the appropriate angle for landing. Don't be impatient: Don't pivot your skis while your poles are still planted, because you might hit the tails of your skis on your planted poles. Pull your poles in by lifting your hands forward, in front of your body. Maintain your proper flight position. Stick your landing and ski away.

Cornice drop

Rob is entering a cornice above the Kitchen Wall off the Palisades at Squaw Valley. This cornice has some new snow buildup from a light flurry with high winds. It is essentially stable except for the new edge. The snow below is classic spring corn: predictable and grippy, yet soft for landing. The type of jump we are describing here is the same one you would use for any takeoff over a sharp drop—for example, over a small waterfall or cliff like those found at may ski areas in New England. Basically, this is a good technique for any drop where you are unsure of the conditions at the lip.

In this instance, at Squaw, the key move was to get over the cornice edge without disturbing it. The solution: a prejump with a little speed from three or four feet back so that Rob could just float over the lip of the cornice, minimizing airtime.

Photo 1: Rob jumps up slightly and lifts his knees for extra height and a compact body position to provide stability in flight. Notice how his left pole is still planted. This action freezes the momentum on his left side, so he can initiate a left turn in flight. His right hand and arm drive slightly forward to begin this airplane turn and to act as a turn regulator while Rob is in the air.

Photo 2: Rob holds his hands low so they can act as balance adjusters. His skis are tipped slightly on edge, positioned for a left turn in the air. He establishes his flight position as he comes over the cornice: upper body is perpendicular to the pitch of the landing hill and skis are parallel with the landing hill.

Photo 3: Rob has pulled back his right hand slightly to slow his rotation in the air. He has realized that the airtime is going to be greater than he expected at takeoff, so he slows the rotation to avoid having his skis land perpendicular to the fall line. Otherwise, with the snow relatively firm (four inches of corn snow with a firm surface underneath), the impact will be too great. It is better to land with your skis at about a 45-degree angle to the fall line and be ready to nail your first two turns to slow down, or be ready for high-speed long-radius turns, which is what Rob is doing in this photo. You would not want to do this if you were jumping onto a face with lots of rocks and trees.

Photo 4: Rob starts to extend his legs in preparation for touchdown. His upper body is positioned slightly back from perpendicular to the slope (to keep from being thrown forward when he lands). Notice that his skis are parallel to the slope. This position allows full edge contact immediately upon landing for a quick braking turn.

A note on cornice stability: Most North American ski areas do a good job with avalanche control, so you can usually rely on inbounds cornices to be stable. Mostly. This is not true of out-of-bounds or backcountry cornices, which can collapse massively under a single skier's weight.

A second note on cornice stability: Remember that it's bad luck to pee on a cornice. Seriously.

When you land in deep powder, you will be plowing through the snow like a bowling ball through the pins.

How to land a jump in powder

Powder is the sweetest landing surface a skier can have. You get a soft landing with a cold face shot. To stick a powder landing, you need to maintain your fore-aft balance as your skis submerge in the snow. If you're too far back on your skis, you'll go over backwards; if you're too far forward, you'll go over the bars.

A "four-point landing" is key: Your skis and both poles should touch down together, with your hands in front, and your feet slightly ahead of your hips. Touching down with your feet slightly in front of your hips lets your whole body absorb the force of landing and allows a full range of motion so your knees can suck up in front of you. The heavier the snow, the more important this becomes.

As your skis float up to the surface, you need to look where you're going. Be ready for speed. In fact, before you jump, you should visualize straight-running the hill from your takeoff point to the point where you will make your next turn—below your landing—so you'll be mentally prepared for the speed. Then make a full turn, getting your skis totally perpendicular to the fall line for speed control and a smooth continuation of your descent. Smile and don't forget to breathe!

Tip: The new fat and midfat shaped skis make this fore-aft balancing thing significantly easier. You can basically land in powder as you do on firmer snow: centered. A wider-profile ski provides inherent float because the tip and tail will stay closer to the surface, so you'll naturally float back to the snow surface quicker than on a conventional ski.

Don't be distracted by little things like people on the lift, your friends watching or your shadow flying across a rock nearby!

Breakable crust

The word crusty never brings to mind anything pleasant, except apple pie, and you'll want that only with ice cream. Crusty snow is usually enough to send even the most hard core ski freak home, muttering words like unskiable and crap.

However, with the right skis and good technique, you can survive the gnarl and actually rip it up—at least if the crust is thin enough that the skis can cut through it.

You are better off skiing on fatter skis in crusty snow. Skinny or traditional skis submarine, and once they've dived under the crust there's no pulling them back up. Wider skis float better, keeping your skis closer to the snow surface and cutting the crust with the least resistance. You never want your tips to dive under the crust.

We teach a carve the crust approach. The key is to match the ski edge angles to create the turn, using a powerful stance to drive your skis. Ski weighting—the act of guiding the build up of G's as your body settles onto your skis—is delicate in the fore-aft plane. To prevent the tips diving, as you round out the finish of the turn into the transition, you need to pressure your skis together with a little bit of heel pressure—while keeping your shins snug to the front of your boots. That action will keep your tips light, staying at or above the snow surface.

Be sure always to have your skis at matching angles when they are weighted in the turn so you can benefit from the full surface area of both skis. This is how we get the skis working together, to create an efficient two-footed carve through the crust. When skis are

edged differently, the crust grabs them differently, and you risk a tip-cross or split.

As always, keep your hips low for
strength and your shoulders centered over your
feet, facing your direction of travel. This position
is both powerful and versatile: It permits you to
make micro weight adjustments (fore-aft and
foot-to-foot) throughout the turn .

The snow in this photo sequence is a lot
worse then it looks. The sun and windcrust is an
inch or two thick—thin enough to break under
your weight and allow your skis to penetrate into
the deeper powder. But the crust is thick
enough that, if you allow your tips to dive, it will
keep them from resurfacing. With wide skis and
good technique, it can be fun to ski.

Photo 1: Notice the matching edge
angles and equal foot pressure as Eric crosses
a small rolling cornice. The skis cut lightly into
the crust. He is poised, guiding the build-up of
G's and the shape of the turn.

Photo 2: The moment of truth: Will he
break through or not? He has a solid two-ski
platform. His weight is centered. Ski tips float
close to the surface, and the skis match for
edge angle. All this looks good. Even so, as his
skis cross the fall line into bottom of the turn, he
has a lot of potential to break through the crust.
Be delicate here! Notice the low hips for power
and balance: If the skis do break through the
crust, he's in position to drive the through the
skis through the crust and into the transition.

Photo 3: Yes, he's still floating. As his skis
cross the slope, Eric begins to release this turn.

The action now is leg retraction to unweight the skis. Relax both feet and legs together. Relax and retract, with shoulders and eyes facing the next turn. Now in mid-transition, Eric is in a purely neutral stance, with both skis riding flat and light on snow surface. He's relaxed, with legs retracted, and guiding both feet together. This is the only moment in crust carving that is relaxing. As Eric flows through this neutral phase, his new inside ski leads the move to new edges. As the skis come onto edge and seek the fall line, the G's build and Eric begins to weight his skis again. The edges match, setting up the two-ski platform.

Photo 4: Just a little further into the turn, Eric's weight has not yet settled onto the skis yet. Already, though, the modern sidecut of his skis are arcing the top of the turn for him. Eric has picked up his inside ski (more for demonstration purposes than for function). He's using this light ski to lead the edge change, and he sets the angle for support on the outside ski. With skis angled together, he is patient. He doesn't need to steer the skis. He is poised to pressure both skis, with his weight slightly on his heels to keep the ski tips light. The rest of the ski buries and bends in the snow, creating the turn. He'll ride out the rest of the turn, resisting the G-force build-up until the next balanced release.

Crusty tip: The slopes start to crust over a day or two after a storm. Try searching around the mountain for the thinnest crust. You're most likely to find it on slopes sheltered from the sun and wind. Where there's been no sun or wind, there may be no crust at all.

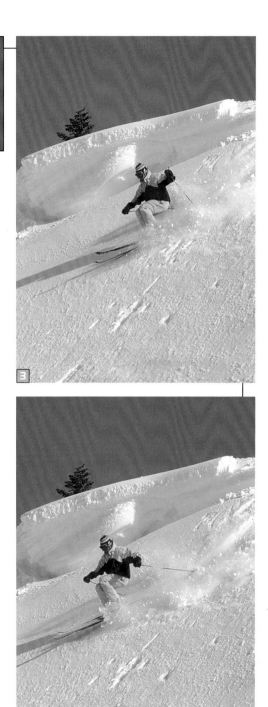

Get the right skis, spend more time on the hill and don't be so quick to give up when the going gets tough. Once you get the hang of it, it's not all that bad! Not all the time, anyway.

Also, on a sunny day, the heat of the sun will often soften a firm crust, so look for sunny slopes and give them a go.

Skiing in flat light

Skiing in flat, low light can be really tough. It can also be delightful. For example, you can expect flat light when it's dumping snow, but the pay-off is that your tracks fill in after every run so each run is fresh.

The problem, of course, is that while you can see plenty of snow, you can't really see the snow surface. You're not exactly blind, but you're forced to ski by feel. Here are a couple suggestions to help you next time you're out looking for the goods during a storm or on a cloudy day.

Consider the terrain. What known hazards do you need to consider? Are there moguls you can't see? Sudden, snow covered drops? Cat-tracks? Terrain variations? Crevasses? What unknown hazards are there on the slope you want to ski? Frosty the Snowman kicking back in the middle of the slope? A yeti having lunch on a huge kicker? Try to consider any serious health threats that may exist where you want to ski. Ski at an appropriate speed for the terrain.

Photo 1: Stay true to form. Don't throw your good technique out the window. Here Eric maintains a slightly lower stance throughout the entire run. This lower center of gravity provides

more stable balancing with quicker reaction time to help him deal with unseen surprises on the surface.

Photo 2: At the end of the turn, Eric is low and strong. He is poised to release the turn and flow into the next one. He will stay compact and strong through the transition.

Photo 3: Standing straight in the transition would put him in a weak, vulnerable position, unable to react quickly. Instead, he stays low and centered over his skis. This is the moment of truth, when the brain may say, "Forget this." Have confidence. Go with it.

Photo 4: The skis carve, as they should. Eric is still poised and balanced as the turn is coming around and the G's build up on the skis. He resists the urge to steer and skid the skis across the fall line.

Photo 5: Here's the control phase. You can see more snow coming off the skis, which means the forces are building. Eric maintains a strong, low center of gravity. From this point he can ride through the turn regardless of what his skis encounter.

No doubt, half the challenge is having the confidence to treat flat light as if you can still see. Keep it together and you can get some great runs in while less motivated buddies watch CHiPs reruns in the base lodge.

Tip: Whenever you can, ski close to visible objects like rocks or trees to provide definition for the slope. Also, wear yellow or rose lens eyewear to brighten your field of vision. Avoid dark-colored lenses, which are made for bright sun.

Don't freak out just because you can't see the snow clearly. Ski in areas you are familiar with and ski a little slower than normal.

Flat light revisted: Trust your instincts

The situation: Nasty weather. Authentic white-out. Howling wind. Six inches of powder on the ground and more falling every second. Visibility practically zero but the powder's superb, and ya gotta have it.

In a real whiteout, it's possible to get so disoriented that you become an inverted aerial-ist without realizing it—until you land. It's not just that you can't see the terrain details. The real problem is that you have no visual horizon for orientation as you do on a day when the snow is white and the sky is blue. The horizon helps us hold the head level so we can rely on balance signals from the inner ear. When the clouds and snow blur together, that horizon disappears, and we can't tell up from down. Here are some tac-tics for semi-blind navigation:

Find alternative visual references. Don't just ski alongside the trees—get in the trees. Use other skiers, lift towers, rocks—anything to differentiate the slope from the sky.

Ski familiar terrain. This is not a good time to go into uncharted territory, where there might be cliffs, half-buried rocks, or streambeds.

Rely on basic technique. Stay balanced. Focus on the sensations coming through your feet and how your skis are cutting into the snow. Get a rhythm going, turn after turn. When in doubt, make another turn.

Rely on your memory. For instance, if you're skiing a trail you know was a buffed car-pet yesterday, you can flow into your next turn exactly as you did the last, confident that the terrain is consistent. It may take you a couple of runs on the same trail to gain this confidence. But then you can relax and go for it.

Be Luke Skiwalker: Use The Force. Trust your instincts. Keep on skiing and enjoy the mountains in all their splendor, even if you can't see them. Your friends will see you as hardcore, and you'll get some awesome runs in.

HIGH TRAVERSE TRICK

You want that stash of powder the locals are talking about, even though it's a very long, slightly uphill traverse to reach it. No sweat, you think: you're in good shape. But almost as soon as you start out, you realize you can't possibly keep up with that group of hardcores ahead of you. Those guys are cruising! How can they gain elevation, climbing above the well-defined traversing track , and still move so fast?

Those guys possess the secret of the long traverse. They know there's more to it than simply skating and pushing back on your poles. Once you learn this technique and get good at it, you'll be able to traverse quickly and climb above the "tourist" traverse track to access even more of the fresh goods.

Begin by just coasting along the regular traverse track to get a bit of momentum going. Then step up off the downhill ski and onto the uphill edge of

The traverse trick can get you a couple of extra turns, like this one above the Chamonix valley.

your uphill ski. As you do this, point the tip of your uphill ski slightly downhill across the normal traverse line. The uphill step will gain you altitude, and the slight downhill angling of that ski will allow gravity to pull you forward.

Then quickly bring your downhill ski up parallel to your uphill ski. If you set that ski down so the that it points across the hill more than the uphill ski does, you'll keep most of the elevation you just gained when you stand on it. Keep stepping and angling, and you'll maintain your momentum.

In effect, you're side stepping upward while moving forward. It is important to maintain your momentum between steps, so make sure to set your uphill ski down at enough of an angle to allow forward momentum every time. Use your poles to push forward with both arms together every time you step up onto the uphill ski. The poles will help to maintain momentum and aid in stepping up onto the uphill ski. You may be doing 100-200 steps to get all the way across a ridge or bowl, so every little bit of energy conserved counts for a lot.

Tip: In a deep-powder traverse track, lift the tail of your uphill ski and set it back onto the snow with the tail in the powder and the tip angled slightly downhill, in the packed traverse track. The wall of snow on the uphill side of the track will act as a ramp to push you forward.

Backcountry skiing in wild mountains represents a true example of the endless learning curve and the chance for personal growth. Skiers: Eric D. and Andy Dappen (left) in the Italian Alps.

chapter 7

BACKCOUNTRY BASICS

Backcountry skiing is a lot more then just skiing downhill. Only when you experience it for yourself will you discover why so many love it so much.

We can't begin to pack an all-inclusive how-to about backcountry skiing into one chapter. Whole books have been written on the subject of winter wilderness skills. But any discussion of advanced ski technique would be incomplete without touching on some of the basics of backcountry skiing. So in this chapter we'll talk about the many different types of backcountry experiences, discuss the basic gear needs and touring options, and then provide a rough overview of what you need to learn beforehand and where you can get more detailed information.

First, we need to ask: Why do you want to go into the backcountry? Why cross into wild, uncontrolled snow? We do it for a number of reasons:

The backcountry puts us in touch with the environment. It gives us a connection to the natural rhythm of the things that is rarely experienced in daily life. A big part of this connection is the simple beauty of the backcountry—the spectacular scenery. Another big part is the glimpse we get of wildlife—the elk or chamois on the ridgeline, the bear tracks in spring corn snow, the red tail hawk and occasional snow leopard (smile).

Sometimes we like solitude. In this commercial age, nature is often drowned out by the cacophony of fabricated ski town villages, high-speed quads, terrain parks and parking structures. These mountain town constructs are not intrinsically evil. On the contrary, we can log a lot more vertical per day riding a high-speed quad chairlift than when we rely on the quads in our legs. Full-service resorts allow large numbers of people to experience skiing and snowboarding when they might not otherwise—and we all know the world would be a better place if everyone skied. But those very numbers impel some of us to seek a more personal experience in the backcountry.

We love the challenges, which are manifold, beginning with the endlessly varying snow

Good friends and good times in the Chamonix backcountry.

Personal reasons for loving the mountains are diverse. The fact that everyone can relate on some level is universal.

conditions. There's the terrain—the challenges of peaks and couloirs—and the weather, which can range from wonderfully warm and sunny to brutally, dangerously stormy.

We thrive on the camaraderie that you achieve with your backcountry partners.

Finally, there's personal growth—by which we mean the sense of self-sufficiency you earn when you master the challenges of the backcountry.

The bottom line is that everybody has his or her own reasons for going into the backcountry. Whatever yours may be, just get out and do it. It may very well be the best time you will spend in the mountains. Just remember to respect the mountains and the people you share them with.

Types of backcountry experience

Wilderness gates: The best way to get to know the backcountry is to start with day trips near home. A lot of resorts in North America have adopted an "open gate" policy, allowing lift-riding skiers to cross the ski area boundary. The ski patrol often posts a backcountry report. At some resorts, the patrol even does avalanche control work on some of the out-of-bounds terrain—especially where boundaries into the backcountry are adjacent to in-bounds trails. When access gates are open, it means the snow safety director thinks the snow is reasonably stable. It's definitely your responsibility to understand the avalanche hazard in the area you plan to explore, and to bring basic backcountry gear with you—a shovel, probe, beacon, water, layered clothing and some food. If a logbook is provided, be sure

Right: a trail marker in France. Far right: Big Blue sinks in the muck on the way to some spring skiing in the southern Sierra. Below: A room with a view.

to sign out for your party at the gate. Obviously, you never go into the backcountry alone.

Day skiing: Not all day trips have to start at the ski area. Just ask the locals who are too broke to buy a ski pass. They'll know plenty of places to climb for freshies. You'll recognize the popular spots by the seasoned trucks and SUVs parked in places that don't appear to have anything unique about them except for a nice-looking mountain nearby. In a lot of places, the day-trip zones may include some car-shuttle or hitchhiking. Often you can drive to the top of a pass, hike or skin for a bit and then ski all the way to the bottom. By driving or hitchhiking back up the pass afterward, you may avoid thousands of vertical feet of climbing. More skiing and less hiking is an easy sell. Where you need to climb, you may find a beaten path—steps

formed by hordes of hikers pounding out the same track. But don't rely on firm, easy footing: Bring touring gear to get you up the hill.

Snow camping: When you throw an overnight into the mix, you also throw a lot more gear in your pack. In fact, you'd better get a bigger pack, because you'll have significantly more stuff to carry. Whether you're touring from point A to point B, or merely accessing a sweet descent for a couple of days, you must consider the following:

Where will you sleep? It's cold out there at night, and you'll want to plan for the worst, regardless of how optimistic the weather forecast. For sleeping and shelter, you've got a few options. Can you find cabins or alpine huts along the route? Are they equipped with beds? Blankets? If not, you're committed to digging a snow cave, building an

Facing page: Need we say more? Eric and Adam D. touring to some hidden couloirs in the High Sierra. This page: A surreal moment. Matty "Moo" dropping onto a steep pitch while skiing the Ver du Plan in Chamonix.

igloo or pitching a tent. Snow caves aren't a bad option—they're warmer and dryer than you think. Make sure the snow will be deep enough to dig one. If you want to avoid carrying a six pound tent, learn to dig a proper snow cave.

How much can you carry? Once you get into planning an overnight backcountry trip, the limiting factor is the weight of your pack. You can't expect to heft a 100-pound pack around the mountains for any length of time. Even if you're strong enough, think of how the extra weight will drive your skis into the snowpack. So little things count. Sane people reduce pack weight by choosing supplies wisely—cooking equipment, clothes, and luxury items are good places to start paring. One of the more popular approaches among skiers to remedying the

weight issue is to zone-camp. Hump in the heavy pack, or drag a sled for a day or two, and set up a base camp. From there, you can approach the ski zones with a day-pack.

Before you go
Make a plan. Where are you going? Can you define a safe route in and out, then stick to it regardless of visibility? Planning, navigation, and the ability to think and deal with adversity defines a well-prepared backcountry mission.

Check the Weather and Avalanche Forecast. Television, radio, the internet and the United States Forest Service all have weather and snow reports. You must know what conditions exist where you will be going. Be aware that weather and snow conditions can change quickly

Visuals of the evening and morning skies are hard to come by when you only spend daylight hours in the mountains.

ITALY HUTTES

Overnight ski touring is a really fun thing to do. You can go very deep into the mountains and, over a period of a few days, you can really feel the natural rhythm of the mountains. One of the most comfortable options for staying out for many nights is to overnight in a mountain hut. It is very nice not to have to carry a tent or dig a snowcave, plus most huts have beds and wood stoves. Very warm, very comfy.

You will find mountain huts all over the world. Here in the States, we have networks of backcountry huts. Probably the best network for backcountry skiing can be found in central Colorado, where the Tenth Mountain Hut System extends from Leadville to Aspen to Vail.

However, it's the Alps that has the most extensive network of huts in the world. The Alps are nearly all connected by huts from Austria in the north, all the way through Switzerland and France to Italy in the south. Each country has its own style of hut construction and service. The huts go from unmanned refuges in France to the Swiss huts which offer Spartan facilities and a basic breakfast and dinner served up by military-style mountain hosts.

The Italian huts, on the other hand, offer a completely different and refreshingly friendly experience. The Italian people really know how to live it up and this shows in their mountain huts. These mountain lodges are hosted by nice people who cook good Italian food, serve wine with dinner, expresso for dessert and fresh coffee and baked goods for breakfast. Absolutely, ridiculously good! When you get the full pension or family-style dinner,

At left: The food and friendliness of the Rifugio Cesare Branca were outstanding. Above: great skiing on many peaks. In the background, the Gran Zebru, where we laid down some tracks two days after this pic was taken.

you can expect a four-course extrazaganza the likes of which you could only dream about anywhere else in the world.

This classic alpine ambience includes a laidback environment where everyone is friendly and you can sit down for an after-dinner glass of "vino tinto" with German, French, British and Austrian folks in a casual environment of good times and beautiful scenery.

Although the Italian area does not boast the tallest peaks in the Alps, the skiing is still absolutely fantastic. You can ski wide-open bowls, chutes, powder fields and anything else that sparks your fancy. I went in 1996 with Hank deVre to the Ortles region of northwestern Italy. We spent 10 days skiing and touring between three huts. It was awesome! We toured with full glacier travel gear and skied on four peaks and many other slopes along the way. Absolutely classic.

Beautiful and powerful. If you see a cloud like this moving in on the horizon, it is a good time to consider heading home.

in the mountains and your well-being depends on your ability to change your plan as needed.

Look at how the weather has changed over the past 24 hours, and understand how recent snowfall, winds and temperature changes have affected the snowpack. How has the snowpack been affected by recent weather? Heavy precipitation, high winds or major temperature changes all affect the snowpack. Rapid changes in the weather will often contribute to instability and generally raises the avalanche hazard. A good avalanche report will give you this information. Make sure to check a detailed report for your area before heading out.

On a multi-day trip, it's a good idea to carry a pocket NOAA radio. When you have reception, a weather radio will keep you current on forecast changes.

With more time in the backcountry, you'll begin to understand the long-term impact that weather has on the snowpack. Know what the weather has done over the course of the winter. What have the temperatures been doing all season? Have there been any major melting or freezing periods? Recent dumps? If so, what kind of surface did the new snow fall on? Was it windy during the storm? If so, it's likely the wind transported snow over the ridges and deposited it on leeward slopes, thereby loading the slope and forming cornices, increasing the slide potential. What is the forecast? More snow with more wind? If you hear this combo, it should immediately send up a warning flag. Formal training will help you understand this. If you don't understand and respect the snowpack, you may become a part of it!

Having the right gear will make you feel much better about skiing pitches like this sweetheart of a run at Craigieburn, New Zealand.

Eat and drink. Eat and drink plenty of water before you leave in the morning. Don't leave hungry or thirsty.

Bring extra water and food. It's really important to eat during the course of your day in the backcountry to replace expended water and energy, so make sure to bring a lunch, snacks and extra water. Dehydration is very bad news, especially at altitude. The general rule is 50 to 70 ounces of water (1.5 to 2 liters) per day. The more you plan to climb and the higher the altitude, the more you need to drink. Electrolyte drinks are useful for maintaining nutrient and chemical balance as well as proper hydration while working out. Remember to drink lots of water in the morning before going out and again when you get back. Never head out thirsty.

In an average day, you'll burn 2,000 to 3,000 calories. If you plan to climb over 4,000 vertical feet in a day, you can easily burn 4,000 calories, according to Dr. Bill Vaughan, the scientific formulator of Powerbar and GU energy gel. Good food and snacks can make the difference between a miserable slog and a successful and fun tour. According to Dr. Vaughan, "energy gels provide quick and convenient energy even during intense activities (like hiking fast). In addition, "Bars and food are best consumed when your heart rate is below 100 beats per minute or less (generally when you are not hiking). And candy bars provide extra calories at the end of an evening meal."

Dress in layers. This will keep you warm and dry. Avoid cotton clothing as cotton gets cold and clammy when wet and dries very slowly. Be prepared for changeable weather. Bring more clothes then you think you will need and bring enough to keep you comfortable overnight in the mountains. You just never know when you'll have to do an emergency bivouac.

Wicking (base) Layer: This is your "next-to-skin" layer and should pass moisture away from your skin. Undergarments made of wool or synthetic fibers like polypropelene are the best choices. When you are working hard and sweating, this layer will provide warmth and comfort and dry quickly underneath your other layers.

Insulating (middle) Layer: Synthetic or natural fleece, fiberfill, wool, Thinsulate, etc., are all good materials to keep you warm. They also stay warm when wet and yet dry quickly. Layer these appropriately for existing temperatures where you will be skiing.

Protective (outer) Layer: This layer protects you from the wind, rain and snow. The ideal outer layer will be lightweight and not insulated. This layer should be made of breathable, highly water-resistant material to keep out the elements and allow your body to "breathe" (pass sweat vapor to avoid clammy build-up of moisture). It should have a hood and be large enough to fit comfortably over all the layers you need to stay warm.

Headgear: Without a hat on, your head can account for half of your heat loss. This means that if you want to stay warm, you need to keep your head covered. The same principles above apply here. A wool or fleece hat is a must. When coupled with a good hood, you are set in the worst of weather. A baseball cap is good to keep the sun off your head and face, but will provide poor insulation in cold temperatures.

Gloves and mittens: Layering over your hands is good, too. A fleece underlayer and a weather proof outer layer will provide the best performance to keep your hands dry and warm in all conditions. Avoid taking single layer gloves or mittens into the backcountry because once these are wet, they will lose their insulating qualities and take a long time to dry. For all-day outings or longer, it's good to have an extra pair. Mittens are warmer than gloves but sacrifice dexterity.

Socks: The same principles apply here, too. Cotton is bad. Synthetics are good. Socks insulate your feet and reduce friction between your feet and boots. They should be thin to fit well, they should be warm when wet, and they should dry quickly. You can wear two pair if your boots are big enough to remain comfortable. Otherwise, in most cases, one pair of insulating socks should provide plenty of warmth inside your ski boots.

Especially in big mountains where you are a long way from home, carrying a map and compass can really make the difference in adverse weather conditions. Location: Italian Alps.

In addition to clothes you need to stay warm, you always want to carry extra clothing in your pack for emergency situations. Make sure it stays dry! The "money" piece of gear for this or any situation is the down jacket. It's extremely warm and weighs next to nothing. It can make the difference between shivering and being comfortable in an emergency. Weigh the pros and cons of synthetic down versus natural down. Natural down (often called "feathers," though that's not really what down is) is warmer per unit weight and compacts into a very small package. But if you let it get wet it loses its insulating value altogether. A jacket filled with synthetic fibers won't compact as small and isn't quite as warm, but, on the good side, will maintain its warmth when wet. Our choice: For very cold climates and high elevations where we know we'll sleep in dry snow, we go with down. In the coast ranges, where we will likely encounter soggy snow or freezing rain, synthetics are a good choice.

Bring the right equipment

Having the right equipment is essential to a fun and safe backcountry ski outing. Everyone in the group needs to have the right gear.

Avalanche beacon: Your avalanche beacon and the ability to use it efficiently are absolute essentials. The beacon (also called a transceiver) will do you no good unless you have a trustworthy partner equipped with a compatible beacon. You'll need a probe and shovel to find and dig out your buddy in case he or she is buried in an avalanche.

A beacon is expensive—typically $220 to $300. But it is not optional. Everyone in your group must have a beacon and know how to use it. As this is written, two types of beacon are

BACKCOUNTRY ETIQUETTE

Here are a few etiquette tips that should keep your friends, your fellow skiers and your environment a little happier:

- When hiking in your ski boots or with snowshoes, stay off the skinning track. Because your boots sink too deep in the snow, your footprints will ruin a nice skin track and make it really tough for the next people to climb efficiently with their skins.
- When hiking in an established boot track with pre-cut steps, try to step right in the steps already set in the snow. This keeps the up-track in good shape. Also, try not to break the steps. Step up off your whole foot and try to avoid rolling forward and stepping off just your toes.

What goes up, must come down.

- As a faster hiker comes up behind you, step sideways off the track to let this person go by.
- In the backcountry, there is plenty of room for everyone to ski a fresh line, so be sensitive to encroaching on other people's space. In other words, avoid the blatant poaching of another person's line.
- Pack it in, pack it out. Simple. Except for your ski tracks, leave no trace of your being there. Pack out all your food scraps, including your banana peels and apple cores, as these take years to biodegrade (not to mention your Snicker's wrapper).
- When you need to relieve yourself, move away from trails, trailheads and other popular areas. Find a tree or a rock and pee there so you don't mark up the snow. There's nothing worse then coming up onto a beautiful view and having to side-step yellow snow. Do not pee within 200 feet of streams and lakes.
- If you need to do more then pee, then it is a generally accepted wilderness practice to go at least 200 feet from any water or campsite, dig a hole about 8 inches deep in the dirt and do your business there, then bury it. Keep paper use to a minimum and, in the alpine environment with low fire hazard, burn the paper when done. Otherwise, go ahead and either pack it out or bury it.

available—analog and digital. The two modes are compatible—you can use either one to find the other—but the search procedure is a bit easier with a digital unit. Get competent instruction on how to use your beacon.

When your best friend is buried by an avalanche, you need to find him or her right now. You can't call 911. You have to do it. And you have to do it in less then eight minutes. That's the time he or she has before passing out from lack of oxygen. After that, you or your friend will turn blue and start to slip away. The likelihood of recovery alive after 15 minutes is practically nil. If he or she doesn't have an active beacon, or if you don't have one to search with, you're not likely to find this person in time—searching with a probe alone is impossibly slow.

Most guides and patrollers will tell you that if you don't have a lot of practice with the beacon, a digital unit is much easier to use. The digital beacon does a lot of thinking for you—it shows a visual read-out of direction and relative distance to the buried person. In backyard searches, Eric's five-year-old son, Wildon, could consistently find the "victim" in less than eight minutes.

On the other hand, in the hands of an expert, an analog unit can be more useful in locating multiple burials. It doesn't have its own simple "brain," so it does not process and choose between the several incoming signals. An expert searcher can distinguish the beep-beep signal coming from two or more buried transmitters and hone in on one at a time.

So when choosing a beacon, consider the likely conditions of use. If you'll use it occasionally without much practice, and only in parties of two or three skiers, the digital beacon is your best bet. If you use it constantly, practice with it frequently, and ski in parties of four or more, the analog unit may be a better choice. If we were to guide you on a trip, we would want you to have a digital unit to look for one of us. Also, make sure your beacon functions on the modern 457kilohertz frequency. Most units

made before 1990 transmit and receive 2.275kilohertz only. If you're buried with one of these old units, no one is going to find you.

Shovel: The second essential item to take in your pack is your avalanche shovel. You will need this to dig your friend out of an avalanche, dig your snow analysis pit, and, if you have to overnight it, dig your snow cave.

Shovel blades are made of aluminum or Lexan polycarbonate, a tough, nearly unbreakable plastic (it's also commonly used for motorcycle helmets). Lexan shovels are lighter than aluminum, but not as good at cutting through hard, settled avalanche deposition. The aluminum shovel cuts really well and typically has a flatter, smoother back face for better use in digging pits and doing snow analysis. To move a lot of snow quickly, we prefer the aluminum shovel. Attach it to your pack in such a way that it is secure and you can get at it quickly. In guiding circles, it is considered good practice to stow your shovel and probe inside your pack so it will not get ripped off in a fall or in the unlikely event you were caught in a slide and then spit out. You want to keep your shovel so you will be prepared to make a rescue if needed.

Probe: The last essential item is the avalanche probe. You use this when your beacon search has narrowed down to a very small area. You then break out the probe, a long, thin pole about 8 to 12 feet in length. Push the probe down through the snow until it hits the buried victim. Probes are usually made of aluminum tubing, strung together with rubber shock cord for quick assembly, like a lightweight tent pole.

You want to push the probe into the snow hard enough to penetrate the snow but not so hard that you run your friend through like a sword thrust. Do not worry about hitting your friend, though—he or she will be really stoked to feel that probe! When you find your friend with the probe, it will feel kind of like poking a nice T-bone steak with a fork.

Your friends are your lifeline if something happens. Make sure you have good ones who carry the right gear and the know-how to use them. Skiers: Eric and Rob in Cham.

BACKCOUNTRY SAFETY RULES

- Never go alone.
- Always bring beacon, shovel and probe.
- Always know where you're going and what to expect.
- Always get a current weather and avalanche forecast.
- Always bring enough clothing to stay warm overnight.
- Always know the way back to the car and how long the round trip is.
- Never underestimate the hazards. Just because you're going on a day trip doesn't mean the dangers of larger scale backcountry treks aren't present at every turn.

Pack: Once you get the three essentials lined out, you'll need a good pack. As a rule of thumb, for your typical day-skiing adventure, where you are carrying primarily water, food, shovel and probe, and the essential items, you will need a pack of about 2,000 cubic inches capacity. Obviously, the longer and more involved the trip, the bigger your pack will need to be to accommodate the extra food, clothes and gear. Also, it is very handy if your pack can accommodate your skis as well.

Personal items: The remainder of your essential gear consists of small, important items, carried for their utility in an emergency. Some of these can be shared—for instance, not everyone in the group needs to carry a map and compass, but someone needs to have them for insurance. Here are the 10 Essentials:

1. First aid supplies
2. Knife (utility knife with blades and tools)
3. Sunglasses, goggles and sunscreen
4. Map
5. Compass
6. Headlamp/flashlight
7. Matches (candle with tin-foil to melt water is nice, too)
8. Fire starter
9. Extra food and drink
10. Extra clothing (layers, hat, gloves)

Touring gear

The equipment you use to access and move around in the backcountry is based on what you want it to do and what you're good at. The options revolve around the three main types of snow travel: alpine skiing, snowboarding, and nordic/telemark skiing.

Skins: Unless you're snowshoeing, you will be hiking or skinning, so a good pair of climbing skins is important. Skins attach to the bottom of your skis from tip to tail, and their nap allows the skis to slide forward but not back. In the 19th century, they were made of actual sealskin. Today, they're made of fast-drying polyester faux fur. Combined with a free-heel binding, skins are absolutely essential for uphill travel.

Modern skins are made wide and come with a great little trim tool so you can cut them to the shape of your skis. There is a little technique to this: Trim the sides of your skins so that the steel edges of your skis completely show outside the edge of the skins. This allows for bite by both the ski edge and the skin while traversing up a sidehill.

BASICS OF CLIMBING SKINS

Skiing fresh, untracked snow is always a beautiful thing. How you get to the top of the mountain is a matter of choice. Use high-speed quads or the quads on your thighs. Climbing skins, coupled with alpine binding adapters or randonnée bindings, are a very efficient way to access your favorite terrain. With a little practice you can learn sound climbing technique very quickly. Some tips:

Climbing skins mean no postholing and less weight on your back.

- Get skins that really fit your skis. With so many variations in ski shapes, manufacturers now make climbing skins that you can custom cut to follow the sidecut shape of your skis. Leave just your edges, with maybe a millimeter or two of base, showing beyond the edge of the skin. Some skins use a tail clip; others do not. In colder weather (and dry snow), tail clips help to keep your skins from peeling off.

- Don't start too steep when you're just learning to climb with your skins. When you find yourself slipping back, level off your angle of ascent until the skins grip again. Backsliding wastes precious energy.

- Stay fueled and hydrated. Take snacks and water along, and try to eat and drink every hour or so. If you're really sweating, drink more often.

- Keep your skins dry. When they're off your skis, stow them inside your pack. If you're going to use them again later in the day, it's good to keep the glue warm and sticky so they'll stick again later. So fold the skins neatly, put them in a waterproof bag, and carry the bag inside your jacket. Bring skins indoors at night, and hang them up to dry thoroughly.

How it's done:

Photo 1: Eric is just stepping up onto the forward foot. Both skis are flat to the snow surface for maximum grip. The poles are positioned well for stability and to aid forward

Traveling a long distance is a lot about efficiency and pacing. Don't waste energy by moving fast and stopping a lot. Instead, set a slow pace that you know you can maintain for an hour at a time. A good figure for planning your ascent is 750 to 1,000 vertical feet per hour.

movement—plant the pole point behind the boots for forward thrust. It is a gradual move forward onto the right foot.

Photo 2: Once the forward ski is set for grip, slide the back foot forward. Keep it on the snow to conserve energy as you slide it forward. Swing the corresponding ski pole forward as you step (right hand with left foot).

Photo 3: Slide the foot forward until your heel hits and give it a slight "click" onto the ski. Then pause for a brief moment so the skins "set" for max grip.

Photo 4: Move gradually onto the front foot and press the heel of this foot down onto the ski to take another step. This weights the entire length of the ski to maximize grip. Use your poles for balance and to make the step smoother.

Tip: Keep your skis about four inches apart all the time. This makes a nice track and keeps you from bumping your feet together, which can make you slip.

Once you are moving along and grooving in rhythm, the time and the distance seem to warp so that you cover way more ground then you ever thought possible.

Snowshoes and split-boards: Backcountry snowboarders have a couple of options. You can rely on bootpack trails and just carry your board up on your backpack while hiking. In soft snow, you could use lightweight packable snowshoes. A recent development is the split-board. This is a snowboard split down the middle to turn into climbing skis, with nifty convertible bindings. Climb on the skis, peel off the skins, lock the skis together to form a snowboard, rotate the bindings and lock them down into normal snowboarding configuration, and start your descent. Die-hard snowboarders love 'em.

Randonée: If you telemark, of course, all you need is a set of climbing skins. Lightweight telemark gear feels natural on the climb. A technology that bridges the gap between telemarking's ease and alpine's locked-heel security is a boot and binding combination system the French have dubbed randonée—which means roughly "traveling across wild country." In the U.S., it is often called Alpine Touring or "AT" gear (see photos of skinning). Randonée boots look like heavy-duty plastic mountaineering boots, with a Vibram sole for hiking on rock. The sole is shaped to take crampons or to fit into convertible ski bindings. The cuff can be locked for ski descents, or released for hiking and climbing. Compared to alpine ski boots, randonée boots are lighter in weight and more generous in fit. If you plan to do a lot of backcountry travel, a good pair of randonée boots is a great investment.

Randonée bindings are much lighter versions of downhill bindings, but what makes them unique is the heel-release option. This allows you to lift your heels for a nordic-style climb, and then

An uphill kick turn (like this one) is an essential skill for ski touring with climbing skins. Despite the appearance, you do not need to be a contortionist to pull it off.

lock them down for an alpine-style descent. Randonée bindings are a lot lighter than standard alpine bindings and much less cumbersome than alpine touring adapters. Popular brands include Dynafit (the lightest boot/binding combo), Fritschi and Silveretta (with alpine-style release settings up to DIN 12).

A wide variety of skis will work for randonée. In Europe, where a lot of randonée skiing happens on corn snow in the spring and the main goal is to cover a lot of ground, many folks are happy to sacrifice surface area for less weight. But if you're going out to make turns in powder and crud and your main goal is downhill skiing, we recommend a slightly shorter version of the fat or mid-fat ski. The extra width allows you to deal with diverse conditions that you may encounter in the backcountry, and dropping 10cm in length saves a lot of weight.

Alpine adapters: If you love your downhill boots and skis, or don't feel comfortable with randonée or telemark set-ups, then you have the option of using alpine binding adapters. These are essentially attachments that fit into your downhill bindings and provide a hinge point for your boot so you can get a natural climbing stride. They're heavy and a bit awkward, because they boost you about four inches off the snow and you have to take them on and off. But an adapter set is cheaper than buying a new set of boots, bindings and skis, which is what you'd have to do for a randonée or telemark set-up. The other advantage of the adapter is that if you find yourself in really gnarly terrain, it can be reassuring to have your reliable high-performance downhill equipment on your feet for the descent.

IN CASE OF AN EMERGENCY

When an emergency situation occurs, such as responding to an avalanche, becoming lost, injured, fatigued, or experiencing equipment failure, REMEMBER:

S…Stop—and stay put (if in a safe place). Don't just put your head down and keep moving. The farther you go, the longer it will take someone to find you.

T…Think—and evaluate your options. What about others in your party—is everyone prepared? Are you in immediate danger? What can you do to remedy the situation?

O…Observe—Look around you and use what you see to help the situation and to avoid further trouble. Check your surroundings and your equipment.

P…Plan—Formulate and execute a plan of action.

Stopping and implementing a plan will help you to control your fear and avoid panic. Remain calm even if things aren't going quite to plan. Control your thoughts and actions.

*This information comes compliments of the Tahoe Nordic Search and Rescue Team, Inc., an all-volunteer group dedicated to skiing and mountaineering safety. P.O. Box 7703, Tahoe City, CA 96145

Ski Poles: The importance of a good pair of poles can sometimes be overlooked. Good backcountry poles aren't exactly like regular alpine poles. First, you need wide powder baskets. Slalom baskets, about the size of a silver dollar, don't do you much good in bottomless fluff, especially on a steep climb.

Almost every ski pole company makes an adjustable model. These adjust in length from about 15 inches to 60 inches. You usually use a longer pole for touring in mellow terrain, for increased power. When side-hilling it can help to shorten your uphill pole, but you have to switch hands when you change direction. When cramponing straight up in steep terrain, you may want to make both poles quite short. On the downside, adjustable poles are heavier than one-piece alpine poles.

A few companies make poles that double as avalanche probes. The grips and baskets are removable, and the shafts screw together to create a short probe about seven feet long. The only problem with these is that they take longer to assemble than traditional probes and they're a little short. For example, when probing a camping spot on a glacier, crevasses could be hidden by more than just seven feet of snow. (Any snowpack deeper than a regular probe can basically be considered a safe camping zone.) Also, in a time of crisis, it's more likely that your pack will stay with you longer than your ski poles, buying the victim a precious few seconds.

Finally, backcountry poles should have a breakaway wrist strap. You need the straps for poling power on the climb, and to keep your poles with you when you're exposed and your hands are busy. But in an avalanche, you need to be able

Be constantly aware of your surroundings and changing weather.

to shed your poles quickly so they don't drag you under, and when you're tree skiing you don't want a snagged pole to dislocate your shoulder.

Know the people you will be going with. A prime component in planning your adventure is to know and understand the group you will be going with. Does everyone have all the gear? Does everyone know how to use their avalanche beacons and perform a good search? What is the backcountry skiing experience level of the group? Is everyone a good skier?

Set goals and make a plan. Plan the day's skiing around the lowest ability level and the abilities of the group to handle adversity. Before going into the backcountry, you should be very clear about your goals for the trip. Are you going in for high-adrenaline adventure or for low-impact springtime sightseeing? Are you

there mainly to descend a specific challenging couloir, or just to bag some easy powder turns? Does everyone in the group have the skills for what you want to do? What's the acceptable level of risk that everyone is willing to take? Is the group equipped with the knowledge, experience and gear for the expected conditions and hazards? Does everyone in the party agree on the goals? You cannot let the desire to accomplish a certain mission override the ability of the group to handle inherent adversity. You need to balance the desire for new experiences with the reality of identified hazards and the group's ability, individually and as a whole, to deal with things if they go wrong.

How far out do you plan to go? What's the destination? What's the route? Does everyone in the party understand the retreat

With good sense and a humble attitude, you too can live a long life of skiing in the wild. There are old backcountry skiers, and there are dumb backcountry skiers, but there are not too many old, dumb backcountry skiers.

plan? Make a plan, go over it with the group and make sure everyone is comfortable with it.

Tell a responsible person the Three W's. Do this before you leave for your trip. This is essential information in the event that you have trouble and a search is necessary.

WHERE you are going.

WHEN you are returning (time and day).

WHO you are going with.

When you go:

Be familiar with the area you are entering. Especially if you are going beyond the line of sight from your base, at least one person in the group should carry and know how to use a map and compass.

Make constant observations. As you go, continually collect and integrate information into your plan. Consciously evaluate your assumptions, the consequences of your plan and identify alternatives as you go. Be flexible to adjust your plan as conditions may change from what you were expecting.

Be very aware of changing weather conditions (temperature, precipitation and wind). Is the changing weather adding to the hazards of your tour? Is everyone in your group capable of handling the changing conditions? People get lost most often during storms.

Observe actual snow conditions. Is it what you expected—powder, ice, crust, corn? How will the snow be where you want to ski? Can everyone handle the actual conditions you are encountering?

Continually check surrounding peaks, ridges and other landmarks to aid you in navigation on your return. Think about trying to find

Route finding in the mountains is an art form. A good skin track is one that is safe, gets you to where you want to go in minimum time and provides an appropriate angle of ascent so that the least skilled person in the group does not slip.

your way back in low visibility. Will your group be able to navigate effectively? This may very well affect the distance you can safely travel.

Observe the people in your group. How is everyone feeling? Is anyone wet, tired, hungry or thirsty? Is everyone dressed properly? Is everyone thinking clearly (if not, consider the possibility of altitude sickness or hypothermia)? Does everyone appear as strong and skilled as they said they were? These are all things to consider as you go up and are reevaluating your plan.

Recognize and avoid avalanche terrain. Remember this going up and down! Most avalanches that bury people are triggered by those same people. According to the Tahoe Nordic Search and Rescue Team, the main cause of avalanches is people entering into an avalanche zone. Except for extremely cold interior mountains like

the Rockies, most avalanches happen within 24 hours of new snowfall. Remember, call your avalanche hotline before going out.

Make constant observations of any natural avalanche activity. Do you see any slides occurring naturally? Are they happening on slopes similar to where you are going? Are they broad or do they start at a particular point?

Most avalanches occur on slopes greater then 30 degrees and less then 50 degrees. Most deep snow accumulates on the lee sides of the mountains and in gullies or chutes where the wind transported and then deposited the snow. A cornice at the top of a pitch is a very strong indicator that wind loading has occurred and therefore you should be more cautious.

Continually reevaluate your route and be ready to alter it as you gather new information.

Here are a few tips to help with safe route selection (up and down) when avalanches are a consideration:

- Favor slopes that have been hit by the wind. These tend to be more stable.
- Avoid leeward slopes where the wind is most likely to deposit fresh snow and form avalanche conditions.
- Choose the least steep slopes that get you to where you want to go.
- Favor the edge of slope where avalanches are less likely to occur and where safety is closer if one were to occur.
- Be wary of cold, shady slopes in winter and hot, sunny faces in spring.
- Be mindful of slopes between 30 and 45 degrees of pitch.
- Avoid gullies and other low spots where avalanche snow will pile up and bury a victim deeply.

The best way to survive an avalanche is to not get caught in one. Do all that you can to avoid messing with one. Be humble and be willing to head home if conditions are not right for skiing. You can always come back again tomorrow.

Planning, navigation, constant observation, constant reassessment and the ability to think and deal with adversity defines a well-prepared backcountry mission.

Hire a guide: For anyone interested in getting into the backcountry, hiring a guide is the way to go. Guide services abound in all the mountain regions of the world. If you're unsure about any of the issues we've discussed in this chapter, or if you simply want to be as safe as possible and nail the best skiing, hire a guide. A guide is good for times when you are feeling really adventurous and you want to safely push your limits. A guide familiar with the locale can do the thinking for you, find the best snow, and provide a nice cushion of safety while you focus on having a good time. Always pay attention to what the guide is planning and doing so you can learn from your guide.

How to learn more: The best way to learn about snow safety is to take a course. It's always good to ask questions of your guides and mentors, but if you really want to get an understanding of snow physics and weather, you have to study a little bit. Community colleges, guide services and ski patrols throughout the high country offer avalanche courses in the fall and winter (see the list at the end of this chapter).

"Avalanche I" or "Introduction to Backcountry Skiing/Avalanche Awareness" is a good place to start. The only problem with "Avy 1" courses is that sometimes you learn just enough to scare yourself silly. With experience, you'll gain confidence. Find a backcountry ski guide or a very experienced friend to adventure with. It will help you gain perspective on your book-learning.

The next step in formal learning is "Avalanche II." This is a more comprehensive course and good for taking the next step to self-sufficiency and skiing with your friends. "Avalanche III" is great if you want to be a professional guide or ski patroller.

Otherwise, you can always learn more from well-seasoned backcountry skiers who have more experience than you do. Go out and ask questions. Be humble and learn from these experienced backcountry mentors.

To learn proper navigation skills, look into classes offered by many outdoor education companies; it is definitely worth the investment. Navigation and map skills are crucial, especially as you cross the first row of ridges from your starting point. At some point, especially if the weather goes bad and you lose visibility, you'll need map skills to avoid getting lost.

Learn to use a map, compass and altimeter. Today's GPS (Global Positioning System) units can simplify navigation immensely, but a GPS can only tell you where you are on the map, and give you direction and distance to a pre-programmed destination. You

The payoff: Skiing in fresh, untracked snow in the greatest arena which only nature provides. Skier: Eric off the Auguille du Midi.

still need to read the map accurately to fine-tune a safe route home.

Maps provide key information on the terrain they cover. Contour lines show the shape of the mountain, slope angles, and other key features that aid in figuring out where you are and where the safe routes lie. Map reading skills include the ability to identify geologic features (peaks, ridges, drainages, streams, cliffs, outcrops, and so on), locate yourself, plan and record your progress, and pull compass bearings and elevations. These are minimum skills for navigating long distances in unfamiliar terrain. An altimeter is very useful when integrated with good map work. In bad visibility, the altimeter becomes essential.

If you are close to home and in familiar terrain, then you may not need to utilize this skill. But if you're in unfamiliar terrain and become disoriented, you'll need all these skills to guide your group back to base. If you can't navigate effectively with map and compass, you risk spending a cold night out.

But at least you'll have your down jacket!

Conclusion

The backcountry is a beautiful and rewarding environment. At the same time, it can be a dangerous place, deserving our highest level of respect. But if you do it right and educate yourself, you can minimize your exposure to danger and maximize your good times. Experience is the best way to truly understand the complexity of the winter environment. Start small, hire guides, do research, study everything, and go with experienced people. It sounds like an ambitious program, but every step is enjoyable and rewarding. You'll acquire skills that will allow you to do things and go places that will awe and inspire you even more than you imagined.

The sublime joy of skiing the mountains of the world is worth the time and effort to improve your skills. Here Adam D. enjoys a peaceful moment in southern Vermont.

APPENDIX

Drills for skills.

Introduction

In this section, we will detail our favorite and most effective drills and comprehensive progressions for building the essential skills and movements we have been discussing throughout the book. The movements we are isolating and then blending together here are the same movements you will be using when you ski the whole mountain.

Although the idea of doing drills may seem foreign or obnoxiously mundane to many of you, drills are an effective way of building your skills one at a time.

Working on one thing at a time is effective for two reasons. First, you can actually isolate and focus on improving specific movements that may be unfamiliar to you—and then incorporate this corrected aspect into your overall technique. Secondly, by isolating the movement and making it easy on yourself to do it correctly, it is easier for you to generate the sensation of what it feels like to do it correctly. This is an important aspect of learning a new movement, especially if you are training yourself. By recognizing when you are doing something correctly, it is much easier to do it again. This recognition and repetition leads to muscle memory, which is critical to making jumps in your personal development.

In this appendix, there are three progressions to follow, each composed of a series of drills to take you through two complete linked turns. The first is a blue (or intermediate) progression; the second is a black diamond (or advanced) series. The third is meant to prepare you for off-piste skiing. The progressions are relatively similar, but there are subtle yet significant differences between the drills for each ability level.

At the end of the section, we will list another couple of drills that are really effective for working on other moves—like pole plants or general upper body positioning or whatever.

So read the appendix, pick one of the progressions, make a few notes and give it a go on snow. Be aware of the feeling of your skis on snow. Identify when it feels good and or when it feels awkward. It is a simple thing to recognize when you are doing something right—it feels good! If what you are doing feels crappy or unbalanced, then you are probably not doing it correctly, so try the drill again and change the way you are doing something. You should be able to do each step or drill in balance before moving on to the next one.

If you are a professional ski instructor, and you are reading this with the intention of incorporating it into your teaching (that's good!), we would appreciate some feedback on your results. Use the material in full or in part. As a pro, you will know what your clients need to work on, so choose drills that address those particular movements. At the same time, remember that the solution to many people's problems is to simply work on the essentials. Be open and try different combinations of drills. However, try to be true to the movements and look closely for incremental improvements in the person's skiing and what small movements achieve the desired outcome you're looking for. In particular, look closely at the skis and see how small movements affect the outcomes at snow level.

PROGRESSION FOR BLUE TERRAIN

The goal here is to enhance one-footed balance throughout the turn, create a distinct transition from turn to turn and engage the new turn in balance.

First build the bottom of the blue turn

(focusing on the essential movements)

1. Vertical sideslip. Stand across the falline with both edges tipped and engaged (little-toe edge of uphill ski and big-toe edge of downhill ski). Next, flatten the skis to the hill and, as the skis begin to slip, quickly re-tip the feet to engage the edges—and stop. This mimics the release and engagement phases of a ski turn. With a proper stance, you should be able to sideslip in a straight line down the hill. An improper stance makes it difficult to slip in a straight line.

2. Downhill-ski, one-edge traverse. Now practice gliding on the big-toe edge of the downhill ski. There are two versions of this drill. You can traverse and glide with the uphill ski held up off the snow, or you can traverse and glide while picking up and then setting down the uphill ski (which aids balance). This drill mimics the balance required to create a carved turn.

3. Traverse, release, engage. Now release and engage the edges while in a traverse by first flattening both skis to the snow surface and then lightening and tipping the uphill ski to its uphill edge. The traverse and release can happen with both skis weighted, but it's best to engage the edges by lightening and tipping the uphill ski to its little-toe side. This move will also engage the big-toe edge of the downhill ski, causing it to turn up the hill. Make sure the tip of the inside (uphill) ski is lightly touching the snow.

4. Release, drift, garland. Stand with your skis across the hill and the shoulders facing slightly downhill, then flatten the skis to the slope. When the skis start to sideslip and drift toward the falline (keep the upper body facing somewhat downhill), lighten the uphill foot and tip it to the little-toe edge—and stop. The lightening and tipping of the uphill (inside) ski will automatically cause the downhill (turning) ski to tip onto its the big-toe side. Drift as far into the falline as you feel comfortable doing. ("Garland" is a ski-instructors' term meaning a half-turn back uphill.)

Note: It is important not to twist or steer the weighted downhill foot and ski. Trying to turn it by adding a torque or twist will cause the tail to skid, reducing balance and control. It may even lead to improper upper body rotation.

5. Linked garlands. Now simply slow down instead of stopping at the end of each garland; flatten the skis so that they drift toward the falline, then tip the inside ski to the little-toe edge so that both skis turn back uphill away from the falline. The turns are all made in the same direction by lightening and tipping the inside foot.

Now build the top of the blue turn

1. Two-edge traverse. With both edges tipped and engaged, glide across hill. You should feel the skis naturally turn up the hill when balanced on the sides of your feet. This is the bottom of every turn, which sets up the release and transfer move to the new turn.

2. Two-ski traverse stepping on and off the uphill edge of the uphill ski. In a two-footed traverse, simply step back and forth between the big-toe edge of the downhill ski and the little-toe edge of the uphill ski. Balance should be steady with clean edge sets (no slipping of the skis). Now you are beginning to refine one-footed balance on the little-toe (uphill) edge of the uphill ski. This simulates a release from the old turn and a transfer to what will be the new turning leg.

3. Two-footed traverse, transfer, flatten, traverse. From a two-edge traverse, transfer the weight to the uphill ski, flatten both skis to the hill by tipping the newly unweighted (downhill) foot to its little-toe side, let your skis drift for a second toward the falline, then re-engage the two-footed traverse by lightening and tipping the uphill foot back to its little-toe edge—and turn uphill to a stop. Repeat in both directions.

4. Two-footed traverse, flatten and tip to

turn. Now create the complete carved turn initiation. From a moving two-edge traverse (as in drill 3), transfer the weight to the uphill (new outside or dominant turning) ski, flatten both skis to the hill by tipping the newly unweighted foot to its little toe-side and, as the skis begin to drift, stay balanced and continue to tip this lightly weighted foot. You should concentrate on balance and keeping the tip of the inside ski touching the snow to leverage the turn.

Finally create the complete blue-square turn

1. Linked turns with an extended transition. Now link the movements for the top of the turn (turn initiation) with the bottom of the turn (turn completion) to create the complete and balanced parallel carved turn. Perform an extended traverse on both edges, transfer weight to the uphill (new outside or dominant turning ski) by lightening the downhill foot and tipping the newly unweighted (downhill) foot to its little-toe edge. Concentrate on feeling the momentary drift then engagement of the carving ski. Then focus on one-footed balance throughout the complete carved turn by keeping the inside foot nice and light all the way through the falline of each turn.

2. Linked turns with progressively shorter extended transition. This is like drill 1 above, but you should shorten the length of the two-footed traverse between each turn, until you are flowing naturally from one set of edges to the other.

3. Linked parallel turns. Now link complete and balanced parallel carved turns. You should concentrate on one-footed balance throughout. At turn completion, your weight should be shared on two feet, then transferred completely to the uphill (new outside) foot by lightening the downhill (outside) foot of the previous turn. The two skis should be flattened briefly as the inside foot of the new turn is tipped to its little-toe side. Remember to keep the tip of that light ski on the snow. Then repeat the movements of relaxing, flattening and transferring (lightening the downhill foot) followed instantaneously by tipping and engaging. You are now linking balanced carved turns on blue terrain.

To set up the move to black-diamond and off-the-groomed skiing, perform the complete carve but decrease—and then eliminate—the exaggerated one-footed nature of all the drills. You should ultimately perform the complete linked turns with both feet on the snow—but with the weight transfers, foot tipping and balance learned in the drills.

As your ability increases, the link between your turns becomes more direct as the timing and execution of the movements become more focused and balanced. Your speed will naturally increase, which further enhances the link between your turns.

PROGRESSION TO BLACK TERRAIN
The ultimate goal here is to make the engagement of the new turn happen instantaneously following the release of the old turn.

First build the bottom of the expert turn

1. Vertical sideslip. Stand across the falline with both edges (little-toe edge of uphill ski and big-toe edge of downhill ski) tipped and engaged. Next, flatten your skis to the hill and as they begin to slip, re-tip your feet to engage the edges—and stop. Initiate the release movement by tipping the downhill foot down the hill; initiate the engagement of the new turn by tipping the uphill foot to the little-toe side (uphill, into the slope).

2. Downhill ski, one-edge traverse. Now practice gliding on the big-toe edge of the downhill ski. There are two versions of this drill: 1) gliding with the uphill ski held off the snow; or 2) gliding while picking up and setting down the uphill ski to aid in creating consistent balance. This drill is effective at isolating your ability to balance, and it also mirrors the balance required to create a carve turn.

3. Traverse, release, engage. (Do this drill if you are not familiar with the essential movements.) Now release and engage the edges while in a traverse (very similar to the drill in the previous section).

The traverse and release can happen with both skis weighted, but create the edge engagement by lightening and tipping the uphill ski to its little-toe side which will engage the big-toe edge of the downhill ski, causing it to turn up the hill. Perform this tipping with the tip of the ski still lightly touching the snow.

4. Linked Garlands. Face across hill and then flatten the skis to the slope. When the skis start to drift toward the falline (remember to face the upper body downhill), lighten the uphill foot and tip it to the little-toe edge. The lightening and tipping of the inside ski will automatically cause the downhill (dominant turning) ski to tip onto its the big-toe edge. You should be keeping the tip of this lightened ski on the snow to help leverage the turn. Advanced skiers should perform these garlands with speed.

Note: It is important that you not try to turn the weighted, downhill foot and ski. Trying to turn it by adding a torque or twist will cause the tail to skid reducing balance and control. It may also lead to improper upper body rotation.

Now build the top of the expert turn

1. Two-ski traverse, stepping on and off the uphill edge of uphill ski. In a two footed traverse, simply step back and forth between the big-toe edge of the downhill ski and the little-toe edge of the uphill ski. Balance should be steady. You are now beginning to refine one-footed balance on the little-toe (uphill) edge of the uphill ski. This foot becomes the outside (support) leg in the new turn.

2. One-ski traverse balancing on little-toe side of the uphill ski (same drill as in Chapter 1). Now, glide across the hill balanced completely on the uphill edge of your uphill ski. This may be a new feeling for many people. It is acceptable for the downhill foot to brush the snow surface or to tap the downhill ski to help you balance to get the feel for this.

3. Uphill edge engagement, traverse, turn initiation by tipping unweighted foot. (This is the "I can't believe it's so easy to turn" drill.) Traverse on that same uphill edge as in the pre-

vious drill, but this time you want to go into a turn by tipping the lightened downhill (inside) foot down the hill, into the new turn. Balance on the weighted foot without skidding or pivoting it. Perform this one turn at a time in each direction. This drill combines one-footed balance and a more direct engagement of the new turn.

Now link complete expert turns

1. Linked turns with extended transfer. Now link the movements of drill 3 of turn initiation (top of the turn) and drill 4 of turn completion (bottom of the turn) to create the complete and balanced expert parallel carved turn. As you finish a turn, perform an extended glide across the hill on the little-toe edge of the uphill ski before tipping the new inside ski to its little-toe edge. Concentrate on one-footed balance throughout the complete carve turn.

2. Linked turns with progressively shorter extended transfer. Now shorten the glide on the little-toe edge with each turn until you are flowing naturally from one set of edges to the other.

3. Linked parallel turns. Now link complete and balanced expert parallel carved turns. Concentrate on one-footed balance throughout the complete carved turn by keeping the inside ski lightly brushing the snow surface. At turn completion, release the outside ski from the turn by shortening that leg, causing a transfer of weight to the uphill (inside) ski. Then tip the downhill foot to its little-toe side. Remember to keep the tip of that light ski on the snow.

4. Linked parallel turns with both feet on the snow. Once you are comfortable with flowing from carve to carve by shortening the downhill (new inside) leg and tipping that ski to its little-toe edge, simply relax that leg instead of shortening it, and tip it to its little-toe side—but keep it on the snow. The movements are now very refined and subtle. It is very important to emphasize the distinct weight transfers that are still occurring, yet not visually obvious. When you do this correctly, you should feel your legs swinging underneath you like a pendulum as you flow from turn to turn.

Preparing for the non-groomed

Now, as you prepare to get off the groomed, we must emphasize that, first and foremost, the movements that create these off-groomed turns are exactly the same as the movements on groomed, in regards to foot tipping in the natural flow of release, transition and engagement. However, there are two new elements to reckon with in the non-groomed environment that create slight modifications in the turns and stance.

The two new elements are soft snow and terrain variations. Soft snow requires more surface area (two-footed weighting) in the bottom of the turn to maintain float. The soft snow is also more difficult to plow through; in a sense it creates a "pushing effect" against your feet and shins as you plow through it. Therefore, you must adapt by adopting a slightly lower stance to keep the hips and upper body slightly behind your feet, as we discussed in detail in Chapter 3. If you feel yourself too far back when thinking about this, try pulling your feet back under your body as you flow between turns and you pass though the neutral zone between turns.

You also need to be ready to absorb these terrain variations, sometimes seen and sometimes unexpected. By having your feet just slightly ahead of your lowered hips, you are already in position to absorb these bumps.

PROGRESSION TO OFF-GROOMED CARVING

The goal now is to apply the exact principals of intermediate and expert groomed carving to off groomed skiing (carving) with its slight adjustments.

On the groomed, refine the bottom of the non-groomed turn

1. Be sure you are capable of, and comfortable with, the concepts and techniques of the "Bottom of the Expert Turn" drills. You should be able to perform them in balance.

2. Javelin Drill. Just as in Chapter 1, perform the turn completion with the ski of the inside foot completely unweighted and crossed over the tip of the turning ski. This will create very dynamic angulation and balance in preparation for the non-groomed terrain. As we said before, practice this on a groomed slope which you are very comfortable with, because you want to able to do this in proper balance.

3. Inside-foot turn completion. Here's a tricky little drill. As you pass though the falline of each turn, pick up your outside ski to transfer all your weight to the little-toe edge of the inside foot and complete the turn on this foot. This exaggerates the early weight transfer to the uphill ski to simulate the sensation present in the two-footed turn completion required for non-groomed skiing.

On the groomed, refine the top of the non-groomed turn

1. Repeat drill 4 ("Complete the Expert Turn"). Build to that point as necessary.

2. Proceed to next section.

Off the groomed, create complete non-groomed turns

1. Two-footed turn completion. Using the movements discussed to this point, modify the weighting between your feet at the bottom of the turn. This means sharing your weight to varying degrees between your feet, focusing on pulling weight off one ski or the other to increase the weight on the other foot. This is kind of like the recovery move covered in Chapter 3. In other words, in soft snow you need to share the weight more evenly to create "float" with more surface area of skis being used.

2. Relax and tip to initiate. Once you are riding a two-ski platform during the turn completion, it is a very subtle move to continue shortening the outside leg, thereby continuing to transfer weight to the inside foot which will eventually become the new outside foot in the next turn. This smooth link between turns happens as a result of relaxing and tipping the outside foot and leg as the turn is completed.

3. Adjust foot position to handle terrain variations. Throughout non-groomed carved turns, your feet need to be adjusted slightly forward in relationship to your hips, but not so much that you lose shin-to-boot-tongue contact. Always keep your shins snug against the tongue of your ski boots. When done to the appropriate degree (and that degree shifts constantly with snow conditions and speed), this will actually feel very balanced. This body position counteracts the resistance of the deep snow on your feet. It also serves to get your knees in front of your hips, allowing for the full range of motion for absorption. You can also think of this in terms of your hips, too. Just drop your hips a touch behind your feet as you approach the falline of each turn.

Your success when moving off the groomed runs is directly related to how well you performed the essential movements on the groomed runs. Poor balance and other bad habits will be exaggerated in off-groomed conditions. Convince yourself that patience and diligence with these drills will pay off. Once you are successful on the groomed runs, powder and crud will become a whole new world of fun for you and your wider skis.

ADDITIONAL DRILLS TO REFINE BALANCE
Easy

1. Step tips down, glide forward, step tips back uphill to stop. Focus on accurate and firm edge sets for each step. Do not slide your skis your skis around. You should be able to leave very distinct tracks in the snow.

2. Step up garland. While in a slight traverse, pick up the tail of the uphill (inside) ski, tip it to the little-toe side and turn uphill to stop. Repeat in both direction.

3. Straight run to fan step garland. Step out of a steeper traverse or a falline straight run, then pick up the tail of uphill (inside) ski and tip it to little-toe side while still moving. Finish the turn uphill and come to a stop.

4. Push/pull feet in a traverse: This is to refine fore/aft balance. Simply traverse and push the feet forward and then pull them back. The idea is to define too far forward and too far back, to find the center and ultimately discover a centered stance.

Medium

1. Thousand steps. For refining balance on corresponding edge angles. This is similar to the fan step drill already discussed in the earlier progression—except now you will step though linked turns. (The earlier drill was only one turn at a time). As you're gliding downhill, step the skis around all the way through a complete turn, then step them around through your next turn. This drill is really great for your stance and for transferring balance between your feet. Make sure that each "step" is a good, solid edge set which leaves a distinct mark in the snow.

Other Drills

1. Hold poles level across front of the body. Hold your poles in both hands keeping them level and comfortably in front of the body in normal hand position. You should always keep your hands pointing in your direction of travel. This is for hand position and upper body stabilization.

2. Hold poles upside-down in front of the body. This is very similar to number 1 above. Hold your poles by your grips upside down in each hand comfortably in front of the body in normal hand position (tips pointing up). Use your poles like a gun-sight and look right between them at the middle of your next turn. You should always keep your hands pointing in your direction of travel. This is for hand and upper body positioning.

3. Forward sideslip with direction changes. For: upper/lower body separation. Traverse across the hill with your upper body facing 45 degrees down the hill. Flatten the skis to drift in line with your upper body, then edge the skis to turn slightly up hill. Flatten to release and repeat, always keeping the upper body facing in the same direction as when starting the drill.